The CAPTAIN and the JUDGE

Building Camps, Forts, Dams, Bridges and Character Across the Ozarks

Natalie Prussing Halpin

and

Lisa Irle

AP
Acclaim Press
MORLEY, MISSOURI

Acclaim Press
— Your Next Great Book —

P.O. Box 238
Morley, MO 63767
(573) 472-9800
www.acclaimpress.com

Book Design: Rodney Atchley
Cover Design: M. Frene Melton

ISBN: 978-1-942613-79-4 / 1-942613-79-2
Library of Congress Control Number: 2017912730

First Printing 2018
Printed in the United States of America
10 9 8 7 6 5 4 3 2 1

This publication was produced using available information.
The publisher regrets it cannot assume responsibility for errors or omissions.

CONTENTS

INTRODUCTION

Courage and commitment to a certain path are sometimes apparent very early in the life of a child. That determination is illustrated in this story from Natalie Jr. (Prussing) Halpin about her mother, known as Captain Nat, for whom she was named.

Before the famous Castle Hotel at Ha Ha Tonka was built, the Wilsons traveled there for summer vacations a bit closer to home. "The trip was a hard one by wagon. The journey took three days from Warrensburg over rocky and slab roads that bruised your liver. But it was worth it, or at least Nat and her brother thought so. Their older sisters were unimpressed, prim and proper, unlike Nat and John who could hardly wait to swing like monkeys on giant grapevines and to go swimming and fishing. Every summer they set out for Ha Ha Tonka in a horse drawn wagonette. Nat and John studied the wild flowers and trees. With a shared rifle they honed their shooting skills with target practice. Boating and fishing were everyday pastimes." —*From the writings of Natalie Halpin*

Nat's entire young life on a farm, then on the edge of Warrensburg, was influenced by her education for nearly fourteen years at the conveniently located "Normal #2 Training School" [University of Central Missouri], just blocks from her home. Post-graduate work at Sargent College of Allied Health Professions in Boston included serving as counselor at Sargent's organized, military-style physical education camping program in New Hampshire. In Memphis, Tennessee, she had the distinction of becoming one of the first women in the United States awarded Life Saving Certification. Returning home she noticed the lack of similar facilities in the Midwest.

Memories surfaced of happy childhood summers spent with her family near the rivers in the Missouri Ozarks. It occurred to Wilson that a fa-

Captain Nat Wilson, Leader of Camp Carry On ca. 1920, in what would become her signature attire.

Max Prussing, World War I uniform, ca. 1918

vorite spot on the Niangua River near "Old Linn Creek" would be a perfect locale for her camp. She would work toward the mission statement to provide opportunities for young women to become self-sufficient.

Camp Carry-On promoted activities that would become a sustaining factor in the economics of the Ozarks: camping, floating, fishing, and enjoying the beauty that nature has to offer.

The first privately owned camp for young ladies in the Midwest, Camp Carry-On, was established by Natalie Wilson in 1917, with a lot of hard physical work. "Captain Nat", as she would be known to her loyal campers, lived at the summer camp and oversaw the whole process. Nat hired local residents to fell logs, develop land, and build the infrastructure of the camp. Nat was the Superintendent of Physical Education in the San Antonio, Texas Public Schools when she opened Camp Carry-On. In her earliest days there she volunteered for an Ambulance Corps that was ready to deploy when WWI ended. Natalie attended Columbia University in New York attaining two additional degrees. She then taught Physical Education at the University of Missouri-Columbia and the University of Central Missouri. From every posting for a quarter of a century, Nat returned to the Ozarks to conduct camp each summer.

Meanwhile... During the same period in Warrensburg, Max Prussing was growing up on a farm about five miles away from the Wilsons. He spent much of his young life working with horses and mules with his father. Nat's memory was that she had seen Max riding a white pony and leading mules and horses to the railyards for sale. Max loved hunting, the farm, and all outdoors. When he signed up for officer training at the beginning of WWI, Max met Harry Truman, already an officer.

The American Expeditionary Force embarked for Europe almost a year later, and Max was a sergeant, having dropped officer training to remain in the field with the men. He was a soldier who preferred tents to barracks and despite training remained with the equine force of the 35th Division, 129th Field Artillery, Battery E. He was "over there" in the trenches, billeting in abandoned French villages until well past the signing of the armistice. He said he never learned as much in his whole time at school as he did in the Army. Letters home document his positive attitude and willingness to learn more about everything. Max moved back and farmed with his father while also attending "The Normal", now UCM. A self-taught surveyor and civil engineer, Max would open a survey office in Old Linn Creek and build his home "Tall Timbers" in the Missouri Ozarks.

The paths of Nat Wilson and Max Prussing crossed in Camden County. By 1927 Camp Carry-On was so successful it had become too big for the rented campground. She found the perfect site a short distance away on Niangua River bend in Camden County. Nat purchased land near her first camp and built Camp Carry-On #2. Max helped realize her design and constructed the camp buildings including beautiful cobblestone retaining walls, paths and steps. Many of the buildings and the springhouse that provided running water for the camp are still in use after nearly a century.

Max, a self-taught civil engineer, was tapped to survey the land for the Lake that would be created by Bagnell Dam. With the original county seat, Linn Creek, now in the path of the rising waters, Max was hired by the county to "lay out" and build the new county seat for the brand-new town of Camdenton. He chose modern city planning with a stunning new county courthouse in the center of a city plan on the wheel design. He ran for office and became "presiding judge," now known as a presiding commissioner. Under his direction Hurricane Deck Bridge would be built and declared the most beautiful bridge in

America! Next he would be hired to lead the planning and construction of Fort Leonard Wood. Beating out other competitive states, the Missouri Ozarks offered many resources that made the location ideal.

Out of necessity, Camp Carry-On would move again, as the meandering rivers of the region were dammed and former favorite beauty spots were flooded. This progress was a temporarily disappointing development, which only spurred on the intrepid Captain Nat to live up to the motto of the camp—born out of the British spirit during World War I, to "Keep Calm, and Carry On." Camp Carry-On was rebuilt in 1935 on the Jack's Fork River near Mountain View, Missouri. Nat would Carry-On with that wonderful enterprise of the Sargent-inspired camp until 1942, twenty-five years!

After World War II, Nat Wilson, by then married to Max Prussing, moved back to Warrensburg to raise their little girl, Nat Jr., and run the family farms. She became a driving force in Republican politics. Girl Scout camping in Knob Noster State Park and at another facility at the edge of Warrensburg were developed under her direction. Max had served the country during World War I and continued to serve as base engineer of Fort Leonard Wood, traveling back and forth to Warrensburg on the weekends.

"Captain Nat" Wilson and her husband, Max Prussing, later known as "Mr. Fort Leonard Wood" were part of the Ozarks landscape as it changed in ways they happily encouraged and implemented. Later development projects were accepted, even embraced, including the transition from the campground so lovingly built and where so many treasured memories were created. During their fascinating lives lived in interesting times, this couple enthusiastically experienced firsthand the history of the United States in the 20th century. Unexpected challenges only encouraged them to re-establish elsewhere. They never looked back, continuing to raise their own independent daughter with love, to work enthusiastically, to get to know people, to improve our world and to quietly spread happiness wherever life took them.

After a front page feature article honoring the elderly Natalie Wilson Prussing's accomplishments appeared under the title "The Liberated Mrs. Prussing" in the *Daily Star Journal* on December 10, 1981, a friend of her daughter, Natalie Jr. Halpin, wanted an interview. The first question the friend asked upon beginning the session was, "How did you become a liberated woman in 1913?" Big Nat's reply was, "Liberated? Liberated? I wasn't liberated; I just did what I wanted to do!!" That was her steadfast reasoning: figure out what needs to be done, and "Do It"! Certainly don't whine about it. And she didn't complain, even though at eighty-eight the old basketball injury, a broken ankle, and a more recent shoulder injury finally slowed her down more than she would have liked.

From Natalie Jr. (Halpin)'s Notes, 2016

Things My Mother Nat Taught Me

- My mother taught me to ride a horse at two-and-a-half, at Camp Carry-On—Jack's Fork
- She taught me how to whittle and make my own whistle.
- She taught me how to swim in the Jack's Fork River by the time I was three.
- I was driving the Farmall tractor at nine.
- She taught me to drive a car at twelve.
- She always kept a Jersey cow and milked every day. She taught me to do that too, though I did not always do it very well!
- She taught me how to take care of my things.
- She taught me how to fix things. Repair don't replace!
- And she taught me that "there is a place for everything and everything in its place."

Things My Father Max Taught Me

- Waste Not, Want Not
- Do something every day, so work doesn't pile up.
- If you break it, fix it!
- If you use an implement or tool, clean it after you use it.
- Don't do anything you're not proud of.
- If you can't pay cash, don't buy it.

This book is dedicated to our parents and others who were instrumental in shaping our lives, many of whom we miss very deeply in their absence.

We are ever grateful for Max and Nat Wilson Prussing, for Roger and Elizabeth Baile Irle, and for all of the extraordinary educators and agriculturists, classically trained or self-taught, of Warrensburg, Missouri and beyond who influenced their lives and ours.

–Natalie Prussing Halpin and Lisa Irle

Young Max

Young Nat

Act I
CONNECTED TO NATURE

Chapter One

AND SO IT BEGAN

In 1865, halfway between the original town of Warrensburg and the "new town" that quickly developed near the "train station" (just an old caboose at the time) along the new railroad tracks, a small foundry was built at the corner of Pine and Warren Streets. Three years later, the foundry had new partners and was owned by S.K. Hall, George Cress, and Alexander Wilson. This Alexander Wilson would have many descendants. His son John H. Wilson and Elma Campbell married on September 1, 1886. Pioneers of the age of steam and wired communications, the family grew to build and become instrumental in the development of Warrensburg and beyond. Alexander's granddaughter Natalie Wilson would be a pioneer in designing her own life's work.

This biographical sketch appeared in Ewing Cockrell's *History of Johnson County, Missouri*, 1918 (p. 499-500).

John H. Wilson, merchant of Warrensburg, Missouri, was born in 1859 in Muskingum County, Ohio, the son of Alexander and Sarah (McCully) Wilson. Alexander Wilson was born in Ohio. He came to Missouri in 1868 and located in Warrensburg, where he put in operation a foundry on the present site of the electric light plant. The foundry was devoted to structural iron work, making cultivators, field rollers, and similar machinery. Alexander Wilson operated this foundry until 1873. He had retired from business four years prior to his death, in 1877. Sarah (McCully) Wilson was also a native of Ohio. Her death occurred in Warrensburg in 1894. Interment for both father and mother was made in the cemetery at Warrensburg.

John H. Wilson is one of four children born to Alexander and Sarah (McCully) Wilson, as follows: Mrs. L. E. Coleman. Warrensburg; Mrs. Margaret Fisher, Marshall, Missouri: Mary C, who died about 1887 in Jefferson City, Missouri; and John H. the subject of this review. John H.

Wilson received his early education in the city schools of Warrensburg, Missouri. He later attended the Warrensburg State Normal School for two years, in 1872 and 1873. After leaving school Mr. Wilson was employed in the clothing business with Frank & Loebenstein, clothiers, in the store located on Pine Street. He was in their employ ten years, when he went into partnership with Mr. Loebenstein, which partnership lasted three years until Mr. Wilson entered the business for himself on North Holden Street. He continued in the clothing business at that location until 1906, when he went to Idaho, entering the clothing business in Lewiston, where he remained two years. Wilson then went to Muskogee, Oklahoma, and was there engaged in the mercantile business for seven years. He then returned to Warrensburg and purchased the Buente Mercantile Company's grocery store, which he still owns and conducts.

In 1901, John H. Wilson was elected mayor of Warrensburg and he served in that capacity two years. During his incumbency the first brick paving in the city was put in on Pine Street and Holden Street.

This paving has served as the nucleus for further paving, which has proceeded steadily. Mr. Wilson was a member of the school board at the time the Warrensburg High School was erected. He is now one of Warrensburg's most active and prominent businessmen. A short article in the Star Journal at the time reported that Mayor Wilson was advocating that all dogs in town be muzzled.

On September 1, 1886, John H. Wilson and Elma Campbell were united in marriage. Elma (Campbell) Wilson was formerly of St. Louis, Missouri. To Mr. and Mrs. Wilson have been born four children, all of whom attended and graduated from the Normal Training School: Estaline, the Warrensburg State Normal School, the State University of Missouri, and Columbia University of New York City, who is now specializing in supervisor's work and is engaged in teaching in Columbia University, New York City; Mary Olive, the Warrensburg State Normal School, and Columbia University, New York City, a children's entertainer, who is now engaged in community Chautauqua work, having made this work her specialty; Natalie, the Warrensburg State Normal School, and the Sargent School of Physical Education, Cambridge, Massachusetts, and now has charge of the physical education of girls in the Girls' Seminary and at the time of this writing is in charge of the military training camp for women at Camp Wahpeton,

Arkansas; and John. Jr., now lieutenant in the Philippine Islands, who graduated June 1916 from St. John's Military Academy at Delafield, Wisconsin, and was immediately commissioned third lieutenant. In July 1916, John Jr. went to the Philippine Islands, where he attended school for a short time, learning the Spanish language, and is at present at NATO Barracks on the Island of Mindanao in charge of a company of native soldiers. Mr. and Mrs. Wilson have reared and educated one of the finest families in the state of Missouri. The Wilson home is a beautiful suburban home on Hurricane Hill, the highest point in the city of Warrensburg."

Elma Campbell Wilson deserves more recognition than she received in this write up at the beginning of the 20th Century. She had indeed "arrived in Warrensburg" via St. Louis but was an accomplished telegrapher who worked for the railroad, her last paid position being in Warrensburg. Born in Ohio in 1868, she was a career woman, whose formal career ended upon her marriage. But she still had plenty of work to do, both at home and in her community. When she passed away in 1947, she had been president of the Warrensburg Chapter of American War Mothers for many years. She was a past state president of that organization, which formed after World War I. "No less interest was displayed by Mrs. Wilson in work of the Episcopal Church" (obituary, *Star Journal,* January 28, 1947). She had been the president of the Women's Guild for thirty years when she retired from that position two years before her death. She entertained frequently, and her home was a gathering place for her friends and those of her children.

Estaline Wilson (Natalie's eldest sister) was born in 1889. Estaline was known as "the smart one." She graduated from the University of Missouri, taught at Normal #2 from 1915 to 1916, and then landed a job teaching English in the Toledo, Ohio public schools. Her graduate degrees were from Columbia University in

Young Estaline Wilson looking very much the lady.

Homes among the trees on Hurricane Hill 2017 – l-r Max and Nat's Little House, Wilson House, Halpin Home

New York City. She married Earl Newcomer, continued her teaching career, and retired in Toledo as Assistant Superintendent of Schools. She wrote a school textbook called *English Today*.

Mary Olive Wilson was born in 1891 and named after Elma's sister, who had married Jim Tyler of Warrensburg. "Ollie," as she was known, had come to Warrensburg to learn railroad telegraphy from her older sister, Elma. Elma relocated from St. Louis to Warrensburg in the early 1880s, after taking a job as a telegrapher at the Warrensburg Missouri Pacific Depot. Elma loved her sister and saw that she had a namesake niece. "Mary O." Wilson, as she was called, graduated from Normal #2 and took a job teaching in mining towns in southern Arizona. She taught in Morenci, Wilcox, and Bisbee. In Bisbee, she married the prosperous Lemuel Shattuck, owner of the Shattuck Den copper mine, Miner's and Merchant's Bank, a lumber yard, and a big ranch. During the summers before they were married, both Estaline and Mary O. traveled the Midwest and New England on the Chautauqua circuit as storytellers.

Natalie Wilson, later "Captain Nat," was born February 12, 1893, on Lincoln's Birthday.

John Campbell Wilson, Nat's little brother, was born in 1895. A graduate of St. John's Military Academy in Delafield, Wisconsin, he joined the Army. After becoming a commissioned officer, he was sent to the Philippines and was in the constabulary during World War I. He was part of the expeditionary force sent to Siberia and Vladivostok, experiencing a very cold winter in Russian barracks. He was owner/publisher of the newspaper in Garden City, Missouri. At one time John worked for Shell Oil in Mexico.

Today, Nat's childhood on Hurricane Hill sounds like something from a storybook. Natalie Wilson was born to parents who taught all

Elma Campbell, young telegrapher for the Missouri Pacific Railroad

John Wilson, businessman, entrepreneur, Mayor of Warrensburg

of their children to take care of themselves at a very early age. Their home on the family farm "Hurricane Hill" is the second highest spot in Warrensburg. Remember Hurricane Hill, so named by Nat's Mother Elma—it will be mentioned often as the home base of Wilsons, Prussings, and Halpins and remains so into the 21st Century.

She was born to a family of well-educated and sociable individuals. Encouraged to be adventurous, she and other children of the neighborhood rambled in a playground of woods, creeks, fields, and barns. She was strongly encouraged to be independent, and as she worked and played through the rest of her life, she would instill that same independence in her students, in Little Nat, and in all those who came under her supervision.

One story retold by her daughter shows this undaunted little girl never felt out of place anywhere and likely was so genuinely charming and friendly that few would question her earnest interest in them. That brings us to one of her first-documented adventures in the world away from her family hill and farm on the east side of Warrensburg.

Aunt Harriet was Nat's nanny in her younger days. A short explanation may be in order. In the early 20th Century, it was customary for many householders and landowners to hire locals, friends and neighbors to work with them around their homes and farms. Often, this work would be done by African Americans who were treated with a variety of levels of respect. In the Wilson family, it appears that the people that they hired became a part of their family— if at a distance. It was common practice at the time to call those like the nanny or cook "Aunt." The Wilson's trust must have been complete, as documented by this story about Aunt Harriet taking Nat to a restaurant that would have been segregated— only for Blacks—at the time.

Baby Natalie Wilson with her nanny, Aunt Harriet Crockett, ca. 1893.

Warrensburg had changed in many ways since the Civil War, but one of the most striking parts of that evolution concerned the new railroad. The rails of the Missouri Pacific Line were open as of July 4, 1865. Now the rails run east and west through the center of the town, but at that time, the town was up on the hill. Main Street, Market Street, Mill Street, and Water Street—old faithful European street names that made it clear what was available in the city center anywhere. The blocks around the original 1840s Johnson County Courthouse were no different. So, when the railroad came to Warrensburg, it was laid in the lowlands south of the town proper. The movement that happened in the wake of that new technology was repeated over and over across the country. The business district shifted to have access to the rails.

Another change concerned temporary barracks, horse barns, and buildings that had been built all around the old town square. Businesses, hotels, homes, and even the courthouse itself had been seized and by the end of the Civil War all had been transformed into a U.S. Army Camp called Camp Grover, after Col. Benjamin Grover, one of the first local casualties of the conflict. Grover was instrumental in getting the rails through Warrensburg, and his family continued as civic and business leaders. When the army moved out and left all the structures, newly emancipated slaves found places to live. Only a block down the hill, the first purpose built school in town—the Howard School—was opened by the Freedman's Bureau, the local school board, and a missionary society to educate the liberated youngsters. So, by process of "evolution," the west side of Warrensburg, with its old-fashioned and war-torn buildings, became less fashionable and was thereafter known as "Old Town." Even to this day when such designations are less obvious, it is the location of four African American church congregations and many long-time black residents.

But back to the 1890s, Nat created the first event in what would become the narrative of her life. If she wanted something, she made sure she got it. You will meet, in these early chapters, the child who became "Captain Nat."

"When Nat was four, her nanny, Aunt Harriet Crockett, asked Mother Elma Wilson if she could take the little one to the Negro restaurant in the "Old Town." Permission was given and off they went. Later that afternoon when they arrived back on Hurricane Hill, Elma asked her daughter, "What did you have for lunch?" The reply was, "My own sweet possum!" Thereafter, when anyone in the family was asked, "What did you have for lunch?" it was the same answer, "My own sweet possum!" *—Natalie Halpin*

The influence of a strong and educated mother, an entrepreneurial father, and their extended families made a huge difference in the life of a little girl who was born on the cusp of the 19th Century. The independent spirit in which she was raised was passed on as she reached out to her campers, her students, and later her own daughter and community. She is remembered as living in a way that made it clear you could be your own person ("being yourself" it was called) and not whine about anything. Complaining and stewing over things, especially things that can't be changed, might keep you from achieving your utmost goals. Nat Wilson had a great impact on each life she touched.

Loved? She certainly ventured forth as if she never doubted it. That loving spirit inspired the rest of her life as a nurturer and educator.

She started on a track… literally, running and jumping her way into a career in physical education. A great basketball player, she was trained in her hometown by the famous Dr. Phog Allen in one of his first academic positions at Missouri State Normal #2. She learned early on from the pioneer Dr. Dudley Sargent at his college in Boston about physical therapy, then called allied sciences. Dr. Sargent was a great believer in outdoor education as a way to promote a very holistic type of healing.

Natalie Wilson may have become one of his primary champions, certainly breaking new ground in the Ozarks while she put his teaching into practice. She suffered through more than one illness or accident that affected her later but never let it slow her down. She was called "the doctor" at all her camps by the mountain folk who would come out of the woods and ask her to come heal their kin.

Basketball played outdoors... notice the basket at the upper left of the photo. (from a ca. 1900 catalog at McClure Archives—UCM)

Chapter Two

THE WILSONS GO TO YELLOWSTONE

August 26, 1897, from the *Warrensburg Star Journal*: "Wilson Family returns from their visit to Blossburg, Montana by train. Left July 5th." Elma's sister Ollie and husband Jim Tyler were stationmasters (agents) for the Northern Pacific R.R. Mary Olive and Jim Seaton Tyler were married in Warrensburg in 1891. The Wilson family traveled by train to Blossburg, MT. From there, they all traveled by horse drawn wagons to Yellowstone Park and camped out for one month.

In 1897, Yellowstone National Park was celebrating twenty-five years since its establishment. The Wilsons may have been interested, because they had family nearby. Also, a local politician, Senator George Graham Vest, whose career in law had brought him to Warrensburg, had recently made news as a protector of the new National Park.

Vest had political aspirations and very soon found himself in Washington representing the interests of Missouri. He was known

A view of Yellowstone from Northern Pacific Railroad advertising

HARPER'S WEEKLY.

DESECRATION OF OUR NATIONAL PARKS.

A scene that may be witnessed if the Yellowstone Park is leased to speculators.—[See Page 46.]

Cartoon from Harpers Weekly when Yellowstone became our First National Park

as a vigilant protector of the first national park, but in 1892 there were so many bills up for various construction and resource-ravaging plans that he said, "When those states [Montana, Wyoming and Idaho] were territories, not represented in the Senate, I considered it the duty of every Senator, as this Park belonged to the people of the United States...to defend its integrity and to keep it for the purposes for which it was originally designed. Since senators have come from those states, who, of course must be supposed to know more about that Park than those of us who live at a distance, and since they have manifested a disposition to mutilate it, I must confess that my interest in it has rather flagged, and I feel very much disposed to wash my hands of the whole business. If the constituencies who are more benefited than any others can possibly be in the Park, are willing to see it cut off, the best disposition of the matter would be to turn it open to the public, let the full greed and avarice of the country have their scope, let the geysers be divided out and taken for the purpose of washing clothes, …let the water of the splendid waterfall in the Yellowstone river be used to turn machinery, let the timber be cut off, in other words, destroy the Park, and make it a sacrifice to the greed of this advanced age in which we live."

No matter whether it was family, support for the park, or just their love for adventure, John and Elma began preparing their family to see the natural wonders of the west. Natalie Jr. has documented their train journey and arrival from family stories:

"Nat and John, stop running up and down the aisles," Elma said, loudly enough for them to hear. "But Mother, we can see the train engine puffing smoke and steam up ahead when we go around the mountain passes. It's fun to stick our heads out the windows," Nat replied. The family was on a lengthy train trip to see the "Wonders of the West." This trip included an adventure to Yellowstone National Park, where the first developments were taking place.

In the summer of 1897, four-year-old Natalie Wilson boarded a westbound Missouri Pacific train with her parents, John and Elma, and three siblings, Estaline, Mary O., and John. This would be the first leg of a journey difficult to imagine today. They would be away from July 5–August 26. Natalie and John were excited about the trip, but Mary O. at six and Estaline at eight would have much preferred staying in their comfortable home on Hurricane Hill.

As the journey progressed, Mary O. said, "Ma—thur, when will we be there? This train is dirty, the trip boring, and Estaline and I are disgusted with the all too common folk on this train!" Elma thought, "Why are my children so different? They are all being raised under the same roof. Two of them love running through the sooty train, talking to strangers, while the other two are appalled by their surroundings.

The train finally arrived in Blossburg, Montana, where Elma's sister Ollie and James Seaton Tyler, her husband, were telegraphers and station masters for the Northern Pacific Railroad. They had been married in Warrensburg in 1891. The group took a few days to plan a much-anticipated 200 mile trip to Yellowstone Park. At last, the family and their luggage was loaded, and all climbed aboard two wagons pulled by big draft horses. Tied behind the wagon were two riding horses and a pony.

As the company prepared to leave, Nat saw her favorite uncle, Bill Campbell, a rancher and a miner who lived nearby. He was the epitome of a western cowboy. He wore a bandana, a big hat, and a mustache.

When he approached he was leading the little pony. "Uncle Bill, who gets to ride the spotted pony," asked Nat? "Why, you, of course" was his answer."

The party of thirteen consisted of John and Elma Wilson; Estaline; Mary O.; Nat; John; Jim and Ollie; their daughter, Arlee; their infant son, Mose; Elma's brother and sister, Bill and Kate Campbell; and Uncle Jim's friend, O.C. Thomason, who also lived in Blossburg.

Uncle Jim Tyler kept a daily diary that chronicles their journey. Beginning in Blossburg, they traveled a while and then camped at the Broadwater Hotel in Helena. They went into Helena to stock up on supplies.

July 20, 1897—Helena to creek near Winston. Moses and Arlee sick. Arlee delirious in the night. Imagining chipmunks on her feet.

July 21st—Winston to Toston, 25 miles

July 22nd—Toston to Three Forks, all are well. Started raining at Three Forks and cold. Missouri folks nearly frozen. Mosquitos bad.

July 23rd—from Three Forks, up Madison River and camp at Riverside which was 25 miles up.

July 24th—John Wilson [Nat's father] and I go trout fishing—good success.

July 25th—Fishing in morning, caught 60 fish. Wilson fell down in swift creek and nearly drowned and lost considerable skin. Moved from Riverside in p.m.--passing Red Bluff and Morris. Camped three miles above Morris at a mining camp.

July 26th—Morris to Cedar Creek, camped at schoolhouse. Killed lots of jackrabbits.

July 27th—Cedar Creek to Indian Creek. Caught lots of fish in beautiful Indian Creek.

July 28th—Indian Creek to 20 miles further up. Madison River— camped on river and were nearly eaten up by mosquitos.

July 29th —Madison River to Henry Lake, Idaho

July 30th—Henry Lake to west end of Yellowstone Park.

July 31st—In the Park. Camped at Fountain Hotel Upper Basin, took in the sights, [Fountain Hotel operated from 1890-1916—Old Faithful Inn opened in 1904. It was probably near the Fountain Hotel where guests were encouraged to bravely watch bears as they dug through the hotel trash at what was called the "Bear Lunch Counter."]

August 1st —Moved to lower end of Lower Basin and examined it thoroughly.

August 2nd—Old Faithful

August 3rd—Camped at Thumb of Lake

August 4th—Went around lake and camped on the Yellowstone River below the lake near Cannon Hotel

August 5th—Camped at Falls of Yellowstone.

August 6th—Camped below Norris [Geyser Basin].

August 7th—At Mammoth Hot Springs and camped near Cinnabar

August 8th—Coming Home, camped on small creek near Emigrant

August 9th—Camped at farm house five miles from top of Summit of Mountains east of Bozeman

August 10th—Came into Bozeman and concluded to send women-folk and children home on train and menfolk went with wagons

August 11th—Bozeman to Three Forks

August 12th—Three Forks to Townsend.

August 13th—Townsend to Helena, 35 miles and horses ready to drop from hard driving.

August 14th—Helena to Blossburg and found womenfolks at home and well. Had no mishaps on journey which was a fine trip.

August 27th—Wilsons returned to Missouri. Kate Campbell remained with us and returned to Mo. Feb 1898.

One of the experiences the group had was related to Natalie Jr. years later. The Yellowstone Lodge provided touring stagecoaches for their guests, and the Wilsons and all boarded for a guided outing. The experienced teamsters negotiated the narrow mountain passes while giving a running commentary on the history and legends of the wondrous area. "Whoa!" The teamster yelled. Another coach approached on the narrow road. Nat and John were excited over the predicament. "What will the driver do?" asked Natalie. All the while, Mary O. moaned, "We're going to die, right here in the middle of the Wild West."

"Keep quiet, children. The teamster has faced this situation before," said their mother. The driver started backing the team. The stagecoach lurched backward for a quarter mile, until reaching a spot in the road wide enough to allow passing.

"That was exciting," Nat said, little brother John laughing with glee. Mary O. was crying and Estaline said, "How could you take us away from our wonderful house and expose us to such dangerous conditions?"

Elma just shook her head.

Nat Wilson Prussing's cousin on a visit to the ghost town of Blossburg, Montana, in the 1980s

After thirty days camping out in Yellowstone Park, the extended family headed the wagon back to Blossburg, a 200-mile journey over rugged country. The teams were driven by Uncle Bill and Uncle Jim, and others probably took turns as well, while Nat rode the spotted pony. Estaline asked, "When are we going to get there?"

Eighty-two years after the Yellowstone adventure, Jim and Ollie Tyler's son, Bill, wrote to his cousin, Mary O. Shattuck. "you have been in our thoughts lately as in August we took a trip through Montana and Yellowstone. We visited the famous town of Blossburg which I believe was the take off point from Yellowstone of the Tylers and Wilsons in 1897. It was from Blossburg that dad wrote so many letters trying to trace his ancestry, and for some time I had wanted to see what the country was like, so this year we went to see it and after doing so I can understand why dad did so much writing while there. After all, what else was there to do? …The station and town are all gone now. It is just a turnaround point for the extra engine which is used to pull the train up the mountain."

Chapter Three

CAMPING AT HA HA TONKA SPRINGS, CA. 1902

The love of the Ozarks was instilled in Natalie Wilson at an early age. At the turn of the 20th century, she and her family traveled by wagon to Ha Ha Tonka Springs in south central Missouri for their summer outing. The area had been frequented for hundreds of years by the Osage Indians. They knew a good thing when they settled near the springs. Ha Ha Tonka means "Laughing Waters" and at one time yielded 140 million gallons a day. Today the figure has dropped to about 48 million gallons.

In 1801 Daniel Boone made note of trapping beaver on Ha Ha Tonka Lake. A letter dated 1805 and written by Lewis and Clark to President Jefferson describes boundaries of the Osage Indian lands as "starting at Ha Ha Tonka." In 1806 President Jefferson dispatched a message to the Osage Indians assembled at "Big Springs on the Niangua River,"

A wagonette of the type used by the Wilsons to travel to the Ozarks.

informing them of the Louisiana Purchase. In 1825, the Osage Indians ceded all the Missouri land to the government, reluctantly would be putting it lightly.

Excerpted from *Country Folk Magazine*, Summer 1998, Vol IV, no.2, issue 11—

The Osage claimed ownership of all the Ozarks between the Missouri River on the north and the Arkansas River on the south. The Cherokees claimed all the southern Ozarks from the Arkansas River to the Gulf of Mexico and eastward to the Carolinas and Georgia. The Cherokees were forcibly removed from their eastern cliaims and the Trail of Tears crossed Kinderhook County [now known as Camden County] and LaClede County in 1838. The trail ended at a sheltered valley near the Illinois River at what is now Talequah, Oklahoma. Driven along by Federal troops with their belongings hauled in government wagons, the Osage lost many in number. Their belongings were lost, discarded or stolen along the way. The Niangua River was called the Ne-on guah, which translates to 'I won't go.' When a speech was given at the dedication of the State Park in 1979, an Osage chief spoke and made clear that 'The land you dedicated today is Osage land. It was purchased from a country having no right to sell it (France) which had taken it from a country having no right to give it (Spain) and no treaty or sale had ever been made with the rightful owners, the Osage.'

In 1830, as the campaign to secure the area for the United States moved forward, a mill was built at Ha Ha Tonka by a man named Garland. He and his business were the front for many criminal associates, and extensive criminal activity took place at the infamous Garland's Mill. Crimes including robbery and murder were tied to the place, but their main activity was the counterfeiting of American, Canadian, and Mexican currency. In 1836, government regulators put an end to those criminal enterprises.

In 1872 the first post office was built, but postal service was discontinued in 1937. In 1904, R.M. Snyder purchased 2,500 acres and started to build Ha Ha Tonka Castle on top of the 200-foot bluff overlooking the springs. Mr. Snyder spared no expense. This was to be a castle of European grandeur, even though he had never been to Europe. He

A postcard of ladies enjoying a wade at Ha Ha Tonka, ca. 1905

was inspired by pictures in books. His superintendent was from Europe and his stone masons from Scotland. The sandstone was quarried one-quarter mile away from the mansion site and transported up the steep incline by a miniature railroad. Besides rooms for family members, there were many guest rooms, a smoking room, a billiard room, banquet rooms, and many others, all facing an enclosed courtyard that extended from the first floor to the top. On the southwest corner of the mansion was Snyder's suite, the natural scenic view as lovely as any in Europe, overlooking springs, bluffs, caves, and river. Indeed, it was a sight to behold.

After Mr. Snyder's death in an auto accident in 1906, his castle sat unfinished until his son completed it in 1922. The Castle was used as a hotel in the 1930s, but in 1942 it burned down, its roof catching fire when a spark from one of the many fireplace chimneys flew into dry tinder. Everyone for miles around could see the smoke and knew Ha Ha Tonka was burning. The Castle was in ruins and loomed on that bluff in shambles until 1978, when the Missouri State Park System bought the property, including 2,500 acres. The ruins are preserved and maintained with many visitor amenities, making it a jewel of Missouri State Parks.

It was "before the Castle" that Nat's family traveled annually to Ha Ha Tonka for their summer vacation of three weeks. Their trip was a hard one by wagon. The 100-mile journey took three and a half days

Castle Ha Ha Tonka, a postcard from Strathmann, the photographer.

from Warrensburg over rocky and slab roads that bruised your liver. [Today the distance can be covered in about two hours!] It was worth it or at least Nat and her younger brother, John, thought so. The older sisters, Mary O. and Estaline, weren't as enthusiastic about camping out in a tent with the snakes, chiggers, and ticks. They continued their prim and proper behavior, unlike Nat and John, who could hardly wait to swing like monkeys on giant grapevines and to go fishing on Ha Ha Tonka Lake and the Niangua River. Fishing was excellent. Crappie and trout, pan fried over a camp fire was hard to beat, especially alongside a pan full of fried potatoes and onions. Estaline and Mary O. would have preferred salmon croquettes and floating island (a delicate dessert of lemon gelatin with a light custard sauce), all served at home by Mariah, their black cook, on a lace cloth covering the dining table. What a contrast those children made.

Every summer the four siblings and their parents would head for Ha Ha Tonka in a wagonette pulled by Tango, the family horse.

Nat and John studied the wild flowers and trees. With a shared rifle, they learned target shooting. Boating and fishing were everyday pastimes in the clear blue Niangua River, many verdant springs feeding the flow. They explored caves, especially a big cave with beautiful stalactites and stalagmites. Many years later it became a tourist attraction after being named "Bridal Cave."

Ha Ha Tonka Spring was too cold to swim in, but the river boasted wonderful swimming holes. On one side of the spring were sheer bluffs 200 feet high. On the other side, there was a path along the tributary that flowed for a mile or so from the spring to the Niangua River. Along this wooded path many wildflowers grow such as Dutchman's Britches, Solomon's Seal, Beard Tongue, wild Columbine, Spiderwort, Blood-root, and others. The big trees hanging over the spring-fed lake and tributary were sycamores and cottonwoods. Growing up the hillsides were oaks, hickories, redbuds, dogwoods, and pawpaws. Everywhere was the chatter of songbirds. All this was bare nature and Nat and John took it all in.

The experience of those early camp outings benefitted the Wilson children. The older sisters, Estaline and Mary O., were young teens and had no desire to sample nature's gifts and surprises. They stuck to the camping area, telling stories, reading, and trying out camp recipes. There were always small children to entertain, and both sisters became astute storytellers, a skill which would lead them to travel the Midwest and East with Chautauqua shows, a popular lyceum and amusement enterprise of the late 19th and early 20th centuries.

Chautauqua shows were named after the town in New York where they began. The local then regional Sunday school teacher training system became a nationwide phenomenon. After the lecture series and entertainments became so popular where they began, like P.T. Barnum, the organizers took the show on the road so that people all over the country could experience higher learning facilitated by famous speakers, spiritualists, and performers. Eventually, Chautauqua shows became more worldly and entertaining, featuring speakers, travelogues, plays, and musical acts. Warrensburg hosted a number of Chautauqua events, and many of those occurred in the lovely setting of the Pertle Springs Resort. Gatherings and conventions of several thousand people were held there throughout the summers. Trainloads of people descended on the town and were housed in tents on platforms throughout the woods there. Several cottages and a hotel were available as well. The rest of the crowd stayed in homes and boarding houses, somewhat like today's Air B&Bs. The Wilson girls were exposed to the events, so while, as the reader will discover, their little sister might have her eyes set on

Fountain and Spring Houses, Pertle Springs.   18.

Pertle Springs Resort in Warrensburg drew large crowds and provided cool entertainments and relaxing activities from 1881 – the 1920s and beyond.

"running away to join the circus," Estaline and Mary O. began traveling the Chautauqua circuit as educators and story tellers.

John's exposure to the rugged Ozarks helped prepare him for close calls and "roughing it" in the Philippines, Siberia, and in Poncho Villa's turbulent Mexico in the 1910s and early 1920s. He, like the others, would continue adventuring throughout much of his life.

For Nat, it was the beginning of her love of camping. She would return to establish the first privately owned girls' camp in the Midwest, Camp Carry-On, located near the laughing waters of Ha Ha Tonka.

Chapter Four

NORMAL TOWN EDUCATION
OR RUN AWAY AND JOIN THE CIRCUS

Natalie attended the elementary school at the local teacher Training College where many up-to-date principles and practices of education were being tested in a controlled setting.

At nine years of age, Nat's gymnastic ability was remarkable. One of her favorite pastimes was turning somersaults while jumping out of the barn hayloft and landing in a pile of hay on her feet. She was the fastest rope climber around and could run faster than her classmates. In her elementary school days, she played basketball at the Laboratory School of Normal #2.

Natalie Wilson, from a young age, was frequently photographed holding the ball. A leader from the first. 1903

Coach Joe Ferguson wrote about Dockery Gym before its first year of use at Warrensburg State Normal School in a promotional booklet found at the McClure Archives at UCM. The state-of-the-art facility would have made quite an impression on Natalie:

The new gymnasium will be open for classes, September, 1905. It contains a men's gymnasium, equipped with the best

Dockery Gym interior, a rare view from a college catalog, shows the third floor running track.

apparatus. The floor space is 75x100 with a 20 foot ceiling. The gallery contains a Robert's running track. 18 Laps to the mile. The women's exercise room, 46x64, 12-foot ceiling is on the second floor. It is well appointed with apparatus, including Swedish bom [beam], stall bars, etc. The first floor has two separate divisions, one for men, the other for women. They contain bath rooms, lockers, bowling alleys and hand ball courts. Every student, unless properly excused, is required to take work in Physical Culture, the kind, amount and time are to be determined by the needs of the student, his daily program and the capacity of the gym. An examination of each student will be made, measurements taken, and his strength tested. Special work, as well as classified work, will be assigned each. An anthropometric chart will be given each student at the beginning and near the close of the work. This will show the student's weakness and how well this has been overcome.

Nat remembered first playing basketball in Dockery Hall when peach baskets were used as hoops under the instruction of coaches Joe Ferguson (a.k.a. J.L. Ferguson who later was an oft-quoted historical columnist in the *Warrensburg Star Journal*, "The Ferguson Files") and Guy Lowman, while Phog Allen was also in residence at the college.

In 1911, Nat is second from the left in a photo of the field hockey team.

"Ferguson had two half bushel baskets put up and offered a quarter to anyone who could put a ball through them." After that, he took her under his wing because she was athletic and she really liked the sport. Ferguson had been her coach at the Normal training school, where she had first practiced her athletic skills. If anyone encouraged her, he did. They played basketball with baskets fastened to poles up high. One thing that was different at the beginning of the sport was that the players would have to jump up and knock the balls out of the basket if they made a point. In fact, retrieving the ball was an important part of the game. Ferguson told her "Grab the basket, then you can reach it!" So, her basketball skills were well developed by the time she became captain of Sargent College's team upon her arrival in Boston.

"Phog Allen," said Nat in her taped interview with James and Virginia Young "when he was at the Normal, that was good basketball! He brought in boys from all over to play. They played MU and other schools, and that was big stuff. Phog was an osteopath who got the school disqualified from playing for a time. The boys lived at his house, ate at his house, did the chores, had their living out of Phog's pocket. He was too busy to practice osteopathy. He may have been coaching at three schools at the same time…. The thing was he brought the best boys back to play for Normal #2."

"Basketball in Warrensburg took like wildfire, so he did a little scouting among the youngsters. Fourth and fifth grade girls played—they were light and small. Phog was a little short fella, he wasn't over five feet tall. I never saw another basketball player like him."

The Osbornes were not just a social and literary club, they also sponsored a basketball team.

Now famous, Phog Allen was the football coach and was the referee at Normal #2's first-ever basketball game in 1905. He also coached men's basketball and played forward. Just a little Phog history here in Nat's own words: "Allen was a doctor of Osteopathy at the age of twenty-six. While employed by the Normal School, the board of regents learned that Phog had been practicing medicine at the same time he was coaching. This was not allowed, and Phog reportedly said he wouldn't give his practice up and left for Kansas University … the rest is history."

Dockery Hall had a four-foot-wide stairway and a racetrack around the top floor, though it was open to the court below. Gymnastic equipment included a flying trapeze and rings. Fourth and fifth grade girls were recruited to participate in acrobatic stunts. Nat remembered "being thrown from apparatus to apparatus, and developing all kinds of tricks".

April 7, 1905. From *Star Journal's* "Backward Glances, 6th annual Athletic Exhibition at Normal #2 Professor Ferguson. The Indian Club drills by girls: New intricate figures—Natalie Wilson was winner of the Club Rose [likely an equivalent to Most Valuable Player awards], she is a very quick and graceful little girl.

Nat's teachers at the training school were memorable. Many of the early instructors had campus buildings named for them and were remembered long after their tenure. In the 1910 *Rhetor* yearbook of Normal #2, Nat is pictured with the Osborne Literary Society basketball team. She is clearly a member of the society but maybe too busy for all the pomp and circumstance. While most of the girls are dressed in white blouses Nat is wearing her basketball togs.

In the early 20th Century, modern dance, interpretive movement was all the rage, and the modern program at the College reflected the renaissance of kinetic dance in all sorts of costumes. The fact that she studied dance very early and continued that interest into her college career gives a background for folk dances that she promoted in all educational settings. Always up-to-date, she continued to modify her practices to keep up with the times.

Nat is top left in this photo from the Sophomore basketball team at the Normal School (UCM)

Chapter Five

A MIND OF HER OWN

The Wilsons Travel to Idaho

Jim and Ollie Tyler retired from the Northern Pacific Railroad and moved to the Nez Perce Prairie. The Federal Government had opened the Nez Perce reservation to homesteading in 1895. The Tylers opened a general store in Fletcher, Idaho, and then moved to nearby Dublin in 1902 to run another general store. Uncle Jim served as Dublin's postmaster. Jim and Ollie's new baby, James Campbell Tyler, arrived on May 18, 1902. Older brother Robert had been born in 1900. So, in 1902, the Wilson family took the train out West again, this time to Idaho. Jim and Ollie met them at the train, and they had a lovely visit of several weeks, but when it was time to leave, nine-year-old Natalie asked to stay for a whole year. Then the Hurricane Hill crew would return to retrieve her. Believe it or not, she got her wish.

Nat driving Tango up Hurricane Hill Lane, 1904.

That year was filled with excitement. There was hunting, fishing, and plenty of time to ride the Indian pony that Uncle Bill had given her. Cousin Arlee was a year older than Natalie and also loved the great out-of-doors.

Watching a PBS *Nature* broadcast, "The River of No Return," Natalie Jr. heard about a plan to restore the wolf population to Idaho, which was assisted by members of the Nez Perce tribe. That reminded her of an organized horseback ride she had taken in the 1980s. Though elk and bighorn sheep were shown in the documentary, she only remembers seeing maybe a bear. She wrote about her experience on the trail:

The five days on the Lewis and Clark Trail were a dream come true because I had heard about the Nez Perce Prairie from my mother for many years. In 1902, when she was nine, Natalie Wilson and family again set out for the Wild West taking the train to Lewiston, Idaho. The Tylers were now merchants with a store just up the mountains from Lewiston on the Nez Perce Prairie. When the Warrensburg Wilsons were ready for their trip home, the precocious Natalie prevailed upon her parents to leave her there… for a year… with her aunt and uncle. The family would return for her a year later. Nat enjoyed a memorable year riding the dear pony across the vast landscape. The most outstanding memorable event was a visit to a Nez Perce tribal gathering where Chief Joseph spoke. He was the tribal Chief of the Wallawa band of the Nez Perce Indians in their homeland in northwestern Oregon.

During the 1877 war between the U.S. Government and the Nez Perce people, over 1,200 U.S. soldiers fought the 800 men, woman and children of the tribe. The Nez Perce refused to give up their ancestral lands and tried to run to the Canadian Border—a fighting retreat of 1,170 miles. The last battle was only 40 miles short of their goal. Over 150 Nez Perce had been killed or wounded. Chief Joseph's famous quotation from his surrender speech summarized the sadness of the fallen warrior, 'From where the sun now stands, I will fight no more forever.'

In 2013 Natalie Jr. Halpin wrote, "When my mother saw the chief, he was still the dignified elder of his defeated tribe. When I had the chance in the mid-1980s to go on an organized Smithsonian horseback ride along the Lewis and Clark trail, I took it. At each entry in the Lewis & Clark Journal, we stopped at the described location and pondered their cold, nearly fatal journey. We had no snow as those on the original journey experienced, and we had professional packers as guides, not the Shoshone woman, Sacagawea, to lead the way. At night we had tents brought in to our locations and wranglers to picket and feed our horses. Half of the 'Cook Shack' was a refrigerated truck, the other half a full kitchen from which we were served delicious meals morning and night with sack lunches readily available at noon. My experience was far from my mother's and certainly far shorter, but I can imagine the excitement of her year in Idaho. The beauty of that trip is embossed in my memory. My mother lived in those mountains and prairies, and I was fortunate to have been there too."

World's Fair Pig
by Natalie Jr. Halpin

1904 was a banner year in Missouri. The Louisiana Purchase Exposition—or World's Fair in St. Louis—dominated the news and the thoughts of all, especially those just a short rail journey away. As an outing, the Wilson family planned a several days trip, going by rail to see this grand international exposition. Twenty million people visited this 1,272 acre site. It was the largest of all World's Fairs, before or since. Arrangements were made, and an allowance was determined. Of course, they would travel by train, and each child would be allotted ten dollars in spending money to last the whole trip. Eleven-year-old Nat announced that she would not be going. She had made arrangements to stay home and spend her ten dollars on an old sow from Old Town. While the family was gone,

Pagoda and Music Pavilion in Forest Park, St. Louis, Mo.

The beautiful gardens, the ice cream, the iced tea! The World's Fair was an impressive sight to the Wilsons, at least most of them.

she walked clear across town, paid her ten dollars to the black gentleman who owned the pig, and drove the sow home with a stick. She had built a little barn for her livestock and was delighted a few days later when there was not only the old sow in the pig pen but also eighteen piglets.

Sisters Mary O. and Estaline exclaimed, "You really missed out!" Upon returning to Hurricane Hill, those girls were full of grand news from their trip. They were served the very first *iced* tea and the very first ice cream in a *cone*. Natalie was not impressed. Nat said, "Why would I even care?... I have eighteen piglets for my ten dollars. What do you have for yours?"

A few years later, in 1906, John H. Wilson closed his men's clothing business and moved his family to Lewiston, Idaho, to open a new store selling men's clothing. In case you were wondering how news traveled back then, *The Knob Noster Gem* reported on November 16th that the *Warrensburg Standard Herald* had printed a story that they were re-printing for the benefit of eastern Johnson County:

"Mrs. Baldwin had handed us a copy of the *Lewiston Evening Teller* of recent date in which it is stated that the John H. Wilson Clothing Co. had opened a fine stock of clothing and gent's furnishings at its new location and was ready for trade... An interview with Mr. Wilson regarding his modes of business is quite interesting. Nearly everybody

Young ladies dressed in their summer whites at Hurricane Hill. Parties were held under a lovely shaded arbor. Sister Mary O. Wilson at right.

in Johnson County knows Mr. Wilson. He is a No. 1 Business man and his friends are legion and it is with pleasure they learn that he is again engaged in business and if good wishes bring success he will enjoy a thriving business from the start."

He stayed for about two years. Then he and some of his family moved to Muscogee, Oklahoma, to open another clothing store. After several years in Muskogee, he moved back to Hurricane Hill in Warrensburg. The ten-acre farm had been rented out during his absence. Their house had been locked and secured. The field had been planted in corn. Their faithful family horse, Tango, was safely boarded at a stable in their absence. They returned to Warrensburg, presumably to allow their children to continue their education in the intellectual and inspirational haven of their Normal School home town.

Nat grew up with horses, keeping, raising, and riding them throughout her life, a passion that she would pass on to her daughter. In her youth, the Wilson's prized buggy horse was Tango. By 1910, automobiles were becoming popular and this development provoked the downfall of Tango. If any motorized vehicle approached, Tango startled and ran away. The best solution seemed to be to sell the horse. Natalie and her family were deeply saddened to learn later that their horse, which was so spooked by the new invention of the horseless carriage, had been sold to work in the coal mines in Montserrat. Horses were taken into the shafts to bring out the coal. Since poor Tango had become flighty, this owner blinded him, put out his eyes, cruelly limiting distractions. It was a sad final scenario for beautiful, high-stepping Tango.

Nat's education continued in the able hands of instructors at the Normal Teacher Training School, and later in the Normal School, she continued to play basketball and be involved in all manner of sports. As previously mentioned, she was a member of the Osborne Literary Society in 1910 and played for their intermural basketball team. There was no formal basketball program for the girls, but the teachers still taught them to play. She left for Sargent College soon after graduating from Normal #2 (University of Central Missouri)

Chapter Six

YOUNG MAX PRUSSING

In 1868, Ferdinand Prussing bought 100 acres of good pastureland five miles east of Warrensburg to begin a successful farming operation. After several good years, a mysterious event took place, never explained or solved to this day. The violent murder of Ferdinand Prussing, just eight years before Max's birth, meant he would never know his grandfather. The murder was reported in the local papers, but no suspect was ever named or tried for the crime. In Max's youth, an "old-timer," Mr. Sams, told Max, "Your father, George, and Uncle Magnus left town for some time after that, presumably to 'take care' of the murderer. The suspect had run up a high bill at Ferdinand's grocery and would not pay. He was forced to pay after being taken to court. Ferdinand's grocery was in the Old Town but had moved to

The Prussing home on 601 Maguire Street in Warrensburg stood from 1880 until 1955.

A photo at the McKee home in the garden shows grandmother Eliza McKee with Baby Max sitting on the lap of his mother, Mary McKee Prussing.

the new business district nearer the railroad at the corner of Holden and Culton Streets.

Ferdinand's son George later added an additional 160 acres across the road from the original parcel. The Prussing Farm started as a cattle ranch with mules becoming the primary focus. George built a 100'x60' mule barn in 1902. He bought 2 year old mules and trained them to pull as teams, selling them to farmers in several counties. These mules would pull farm machinery to plow, plant, mow, harvest, and haul. He also showed fine mules at fairs, winning many ribbons. A number of his mules were sold to the U.S. Government for overseas service in World War I.

Max McKee Prussing was born November 12, 1895 to Mary McKee and George S. Prussing at the Ferdinand Prussing Home at 601 North Maguire Street. The Prussings owned what is now the UCM Prussing Research farm five miles east of town but lived in town so their children could attend the public schools of Warrensburg. Nat would watch Max go by on a white pony, leading packs of mules down to the Missouri Pacific station for sale and shipping. Max's sisters were Louise and Leah Pearl Prussing. His youth, spent in the same idyllic era as Nat's, was less geared to travel. Max was raised doing hard work on the family farm operation including a thriving trade in horses and mules.

March 1902

Dear Mamma, I love you very much and my little sisters, too. I think I will go to Sunday School. I got a 100 today for spelling. Your Max

The Prussing Barn (with doors wide open), ca. 1917... hand built, to last.

In 1904, when the Wilsons, well, most of them, were travelling to the World's Fair in St. Louis, many people stayed home working, just like little Nat Wilson had. By October of that year, many of the over 20,000,000 people who were estimated to have attended the Fair would pass through Warrensburg. Crops were being harvested, and garden produce preserved for the coming winter. Produce of Johnson County and well-cared-for livestock were on display at the Fair at this time of year. Many states would have had their own halls for a World's Fair so close to home.

But for most, life went back to normal. The children returned to school, including nine-year-old Max Prussing. Like many children at this time when almost all of America was engaged in farming, Max and his sisters lived in town in order to attend school. They lived with their McKee aunties on Market Street and sometimes with Aunt Agnes Prussing on Maguire Street. Both homes were within easy walking distance to the school. It was that fall that young Max would have an experience he would always remember. It was on October 10th that a famous head-on collision of two trains would occur in the Bear Creek bottoms on the east side of town. Many articles and a book have been written about the incident. The Johnson County Historical Society has a collection of photos documenting the terrible day. A train coming from Kansas with World's Fair passengers, was divided into two sections employing an additional locomotive before reaching Johnson

A few fine Prussing Mules in 1917, south of Montserrat Park Road

County, Missouri. Miscommunications were responsible and perhaps a sleeping crew on the westbound freight train who did not know of the additional oncoming train. Telegraph operators relayed messages between Warrensburg and Sedalia, saying "There will be a wreck." But there was no way to warn the trains of the inevitable collision. At 4:10 a.m. the two trains collided in the blackness of the countryside miles from any town. The two crews, realizing they were about to collide, set their emergency brakes and jumped, which was company policy.

It seems like quite a distance to walk children over hill and dale and creek and bramble to see a train wreck, but it was also about the same distance Max rode with his father almost daily to care for their farm.

The engines met, with such force that the Missouri Pacific passenger engine shot underneath the freight, causing it to land on the first passenger car. Boiling water and steam poured from the power plants of each engine. Shortly after the crash, which killed thirty people and wounded many others, the word spread and makeshift hospitals and mortuaries would be set up to cope with the horrors. It would be hours before many of the injured were taken to hospitals in Sedalia and Warrensburg. Missouri Pacific backed trains in from the two towns to take out the injured and remove bodies. As word spread, it was estimated nearly 3,000 people from surrounding communities gathered at the crash site to help and gawk, including one teacher who took his students on a field trip to view the carnage. That was Max's teacher. And

An image of the head on collision of two trains near Warrensburg where Max was taken on an impromptu school field trip.

he saw the whole thing as the communities came together to help whoever they could and to tend to those who were beyond help. This gives a bit of insight into the difference a hundred years and instant communications have made in the behavior of those responding to accidents.

Only one crewmember died, a brakeman on the passenger train caught between cars when the trains hit. Many accounts of the accident tell of the horrible carnage. Those not crushed or mangled by pieces of the shattered rail car were scalded to death by steam escaping from the freight locomotive resting on top of them.

The scene of the wreck was on the downgrade, on either side of which there was a steep rise. Both trains had put on extra steam to carry them up the opposite hill, and when they met at the curve at the lowest point, they were running at a terrific rate.

When the trains met, the heavy freight train pushed the passenger engine back into the first coach. The tender of the passenger engine literally cut the coach in two in the center and never stopped until it had plowed itself halfway through the car and its passengers, killing those in the forward end instantly and mangling all within reach in a most horrible manner.

Half a dozen who were not killed outright were so terribly injured that they died before they could be removed from the debris. Many of the dead were almost unrecognizable. Arms and legs were dismembered in several cases and, together with baggage and pieces of wreckage, were tumbled together into a confused mass of bleeding human forms.

The next two coaches were badly damaged, seats being torn up and windows smashed, but in these cars the passengers fared better, all except a few escaping with slight injuries. The Pullman remained upright, and none of its occupants was hurt beyond sustaining a shake-up.

Max is known to have attended the Kemper School when his family resided on Maguire Street in Warrensburg. The Kemper School was one of four ward schools in the town of Warrensburg–the public schools. Kemper was renamed as Pershing School after World War I. It has been the site of Pershing Court Apartments since the demise of the two-story brick building when the school district was modernized in the 1950s.

Max's young life was spent working with his father on the farm, raising and training fine horses and mules, hunting, fishing, and living a healthy country life. As a youngster, he was well known as the boy responsible enough to ride by on a white pony, leading his family's stock for sale at the railyards.

Early in 1917, Max's Uncle Magnus Prussing, a dairy operator, died and left a widow and three small children. Max took over the operation, milking twice a day and delivering the milk to customers. He also found a buyer for the dairy. The location was the northeast corner of the intersection of Business 13 and U.S. 50 Highway. Max commented to his daughter a few years before he died, "That was the only job I ever really disliked. There were not enough hours in the day."

Looks like Max and his best friend are ready for some hunting.

Chapter Seven

NAT'S CONTINUING EDUCATION "BACK EAST"

From the 2017 Sargent website:

Imagine a time when building or strengthening the body was considered beneath the dignity of educated men—much less women, who rarely received higher education. Dr. Dudley Allen Sargent, a 19th-century educator, visionary, and inventor, helped change that belief for good. By emphasizing training for all students, not just athletes, he largely created the discipline of physical education.

Dr. Sargent founded the Sargent School of Physical Training in Cambridge, Massachusetts, in 1881. He also built a reputation as an innovator by developing exercise machines that even weak and disabled individuals could use, thanks to pulley systems with adjustable weights. At his Sargent School, students learned training techniques to strengthen and improve the physical abilities of all people. Dr. Sargent's college became part of Boston University in 1929, five years after his death.

Sargent school on a snowy day.

Sargent School of Physical Education and Allied Sciences was Nat's school of choice, as it was one of only two schools in the country that trained women to become physical education teachers. She attended from 1911-13. The founder of the College was Dr. Dudley A. Sargent. His qualifications listed in the College catalog, the string of letters after his name, and his accomplishments and positions are very impressive: A.M., M.D., S.D., M.P.E.; President, Lecturer on applied Anatomy, Anthropometry, The Philosophy of Education, and the General Theory and Practice of Physical Training. He was also Director of the Hemenway Gymnasium, Harvard University, and the Harvard Summer School for Physical Education.

The introduction to the 1912 Sargent School for Physical Education catalogue gives this history:

> The establishment of the Hemenway Gymnasium at Harvard University in 1880 and the introduction of a new system of apparatus and new methods of instruction created a demand at other colleges and schools for better gymnasiums, equipped with similar appliances, and for teachers qualified to superintend them. Among the first of the institutions to feel the need of a building for physical training was the Society for the Collegiate Instruction of Women, familiarly known as the "Harvard Annex," now Radcliffe College. To fill this want the Sanatory Gymnasium was opened in 1881 by Dr. Sargent, and equipped with the same apparatus.

A new building was completed just before Nat's arrival in Boston, "made of brick and mill framing, is 80 feet in length by 50 feet in width and is five stories in height." The building offered two independent gymnasiums, several locker rooms, shower baths, a swimming tank, a running track, a sun parlor, an office, an examining room, a reception room, and two galleries for special apparatus. The two gyms were equipped with the most approved pieces of German and Swedish heavy apparatus, a complete outfit of all forms of light and portable apparatus, and some thirty or forty of Dr. Sargent's developing apparatus.

"One of the principal objects of this school is to drill young men and women in the theory and practice of physical training in its broadest application and to prepare them to teach in this much neglected branch of education."

As evidence of its progressive methods, the School also pointed with pride to the fact that it was "the first in America to correlate the mental and physical sciences into one curriculum; the first to recognize the merits of the Gilbert system of Classic Dancing and introduce it into coursework; the first to introduce a modified form of Athletics, Military Drill, Basketball and Field Hockey for women; the first to develop treatment of remedial and corrective cases; and the first to invent and prescribe gymnasium games for specific effects, and to institute a course for Playground Teachers."

The school operated several departments. The Normal Department was dedicated to training teachers to understand the whole "human machine upon which she is to work." The Remedial Department focused on healing "the feeble, or those otherwise in need of correction." Also included were treating convalescents, weight gain or loss, and correcting weaknesses or deformities. There was also a Spinal Curvature clinic. Personal Hygiene encompassed modifiable aspects of life (air, diet, exercise, sleep, cleanliness) that teachers could encourage students to improve in their own lives. School Hygiene, Domestic Hygiene, and Occupational Hygiene each had their own departments.

The Recreative Department provided *"a system of recreative and developing exercises for those who wish to enjoy healthful living, to build up their physique and to keep themselves in a vigorous working condition. Much of this work is given through fancy dancing, gym games, and light competitive sports which interest and amuse as well as invigorate the participant."*

Captain Nat, holding the Sargent Basketball in her feet for the photo.

Under "Press Notices" in her keepsake book from a March 2, 1913 unknown newspaper:

Nat noted that the photo was taken at Swampscott, Massachusetts outside the high school there. A section of the article subtitled "Sargent's Excellent Showing" says, "Sargent has not lost a game this Winter. Captain Natalie Wilson who plays center, is confident that the team will finish the season without being defeated." The girls were not only going around to area high schools to play exhibition games, but they were also coaching the high school girls' teams and encouraging intermural matches.

Nat's previous basketball success and height led to her

OLIVER AMES GIRLS OUT WITH CHALLENGE

Want to Play Phillips Post-Season Game---Boys' Title in Doubt.

MISS NATALIE WILSON,
Captain of the Sargent School Basket-Ball Team.

Captain Nat is featured in a news story in a local Boston newspaper.

being chosen captain of the team. The basketball team played most of their games at home against their own with the team divided in half. Occasionally, as the team was so accomplished, they would play exhibition games against Wellesley, Radcliffe, and Brown. Sightseeing was possible around New England during weekends when the team played at high schools in the area.

Though teased about her Southern accent, Nat adjusted quickly to life in new surroundings. Classmates, she reported, "stole her hair ribbons and tried to throw her in a swim tank." She would do flips in the air. When she got to Sargent, they asked, "Why did you come here? You should have joined the circus!" Her antics and acrobatics nearly got her kicked out of the wall scaling program. That must have been one of her favorite activities, later incorporated into her camps and schools.

Early in the program, Nat was instructed to fall into a net from some height. She was 5'9" and weighed 110 lbs. Instead of just falling, she did a flip and landed on her feet like she'd always done in the barn onto the haystack. The coach remarked, "Here's one for our team." She was chosen to climb a tower of fellow students to hang by her knees from a balcony rail at Sargent about twelve feet high. That made her the top step of a ladder of girls who would all have reached the balcony by crawling up and over each other to the hanging girl, who would have to lift them, so they could achieve the balcony rail. As the first person, Nat was thrown above the heads of her team to reach the railing. Her first response, she said in the Young Interview, to being ordered to hang by her knees was "'the hell I will.' But that's how it ended up happening. Another girl would follow and sit on my feet."

This team of girls went on tour to give climbing demonstrations where the whole team would scale a wall in twenty-three seconds. For this feat a special climbing wall was erected with a platform at the top and ladders going up. A girl would be carried down on the front of the ladder while more girls returned to the platform on the underside. Quite a spectacle was enjoyed by the audiences at these exhibitions of strength and skill. In fact, it was almost like being at a circus.

At Sargent, Nat took a course in Corrective Gymnastics, spending a year interning at the Boston Children's Hospital. Part of the gymnastics program was a course in "gait training." In 1912, Natalie Wilson appeared in a local paper in a photographic essay, something new at the time. In the article Professor Sargent's work on posture was highlighted, and several girls were pictured showing different styles of walking. The headline reads "Should Walk to Gain Beauty and Health Told by Professor Sargent." Featured is a determined Nat depicted striding along with the French Army Gait. Others pictured were The Society Hobble Skirt Gait, The Heel and Toe Walk, and the Cross Country Gait. No further information was found with this article

Much of the fall semester found the students at Sargent's 250-acre training camp for young women aged twelve to twenty-four in New Hampshire on Half Moon Lake and over 1000 feet above the sea, two miles from the town of Hancock. The lake was controlled by the camp and offered ample opportunities for all kinds of water sports, though it was small enough to be carefully supervised. Mountain hikes and canoe trips on the Nubanusit and Contoocook rivers were close enough for pleasant outings.

Dr. Dudley Sargent himself was one of Nat's teachers and had a controlling hand in what was at that time his private school. Sargent was a big believer in fresh air and exercise in the outdoors. He writes in an early camp booklet of the unwholesome effects of city life on "children, with their pale faces, feeble digestion and emaciated limbs" in need of the healthy effects of his camp. In a later brochure for the camp, one of Sargent's measurement techniques was described. When a child arrived at camp, a photograph would be taken from the side, showing his or her posture and physique. The photo would be turned into a silhouette, and then compared to the form of the child after several weeks of exercise in the fresh air. An illustration in the brochure stressed the remarkable difference in the straight and confident form of the child after camp.

At the completion of camp, tests were given in "archery, golf, aquatics, athletics and horseback riding, bringing out those mental, moral and neuromuscular qualities which it is the aim of physical education

Nat, on left, demonstrates the French Army Gait in a story featuring Dr. Sargent.

The main camp house at Sargent's Summer Camp where all students put their training to the test.

to develop." Nat took classes at Sargent in dancing, massage, fencing, Indian clubs, first aid, and many other subjects.

Natalie graduated in 1913, and her name was printed in a list from the *Cambridge Tribune.*

In her keepsake book *The Girl Graduate*, a few of her teachers signed including:

D.A. Sargent; Bertel G. Willard [Bertel Glidden Willard, A.D., Instructor in Voice Cultivation and director of Sargent Glee Club]; Harry Clark; George Dearborn [George Van Ness Dearborn, A.M., M.D., Ph.D., Lecturer and Instructor in the Relations of Body and Mind and in the Physiology of Exercise, Professor of Physiology at Tufts College Medical and Dental Schools]; and Elizabeth Andrews [Instructor in Evening Classes and Assistant Instructor in Classic Dancing].

This collection of names provides a small sample of the varied course offerings available to Miss Wilson and, possibly, some of the teachers with whom she was most familiar.

Late in the book, on page 142 under "Jokes and Frolics," there is a wonderfully candid photo of Dr. D. A. Sargent in for a swim.

Candidates for a full certificate, such as Nat received, were required to pass examinations in a sufficient number of subjects in Theory and Practice to receive a total credit of 400 points. A certain number of points are allotted to each subject. The highest mark allotted to any subject is AA, which will be given for excellent work only and implies long experience in teaching the subject. Very good work will receive A; good work will receive B; fair work C.; D will denote simply a passing grade. The course takes three years unless the student wishes to receive credit for work done at other schools in which case those certificates and statements of amount and the character of work done will be considered. The points may be acquired in 2 years by students of rare attainments and marked ability.

The full Normal Course in Theory and Practice was $150 a year.

The following events were recorded in *The Girl Graduate* scrapbook with programs and other mementos kept. Besides the academic and athletic pursuits, the Sargent entertainment calendar was full with the girls attending dances and entertainments, both at the school and on the town.

According to a "Dance Programme" from the Sargent College Dance Dec. 12, 2012. Nat danced with Blake, Flanders, and Foster (twice). [Also called a dance card, this social convention was given out at dances, sometimes attached to the menu or program of entertainment. It had several lines, and sometimes came with a small pencil. Each girl would keep track of her dance partners of the evening.]

An annual vaudeville performance was presented by the Athletic Association of Sargent Normal School. Nat notes in the margin "Good Show." The next year's program lists her on the committee and as performing in "The Sargent School Calendar—in eight scenes representing eight school months given by the (twelve) girls of the Sargent School

A photo taken by Nat of her teacher Dr. Sargent in swimming gear.

Always daring, Nat brings along her friend to walk along the top of a picket fence.

Dormitory. In this order, beginning in October: Registration Day, Initiation, Meet, Basket-Ball [we are confident this is where Nat came in], Mid-Year Examinations, Vaudeville, Spring Activities, Campers say Good-bye to Seniors."

Excerpts from *Cambridge Tribune*, Volume XXXVI, Number 13, 24 May 1913 — Sargent School Exhibiton.

Pupils of the Sargent School for Physical Education gave their annual exhibition of athletics, games, dancing and gymnastics in the Boston Arena on Saturday evening. The crowd was so large that standing room was hard to find and the applause was generous. Young women of all three classes took part in the exhibition and not the least interesting features were the competitive exercises in two of which the freshmen came out winners. The severest contest came in the scaling of a 12 foot wall, where teams of 12 young women, each representing a class tried to see which team could scale the wall in the shortest time... The evening's programme afforded a great deal of variety. The vaulting exercises and the fire escape drill gave a touch of excitement. Using a high horse and a spring board, the young women did all sorts of hair-raising stunts, ending with a run handspring and dive combination that brought even those with seats jump to their feet. In the fire escape drill a number of the young women jumped off a balcony, about 15 feet, into a canvas net held by 30 of their comrades...

A novel part of the exhibition was that devoted to games. While groups of young women played skip-rope, passed a pushball and romped at various children's games, the basket-ball team and a scrub team gave a short but snappy exhibition at one end of the hall. Sarah Lapham '13, Ruth Bailey '13, Natalie Wilson '13 [and others] were cheered heartily.

Under "Special Events" in the keepsake book are a few clippings of memorable outings with the Sargent ladies, including an article from some local paper with a photo about the

Nat with friends in her Sargent School Letter sweater.

Sargent Girls: "Toboggans and Skis Brought out and Winter Sport is Fine" at the "Slide at Franklin Park."

Five girls from Sargent, Nat at Left, at a Field Hockey day.

Chapter Eight

BECOMING CAPTAIN NAT

Soon after her return to Warrensburg from Sargent in 1913, Natalie and her brother John opened a dancing school in Warrensburg. On April 17, 1915, they returned on the train from a trip to Kansas City where they had been learning the latest dance steps.

When they returned, they walked straight home, only later that evening realizing that the Normal School, just a few blocks away, was in flames. The original campus of Nat's alma mater was destroyed save one building, Dockery Hall.

In the summer of 1915, Miss Wilson spent time as an intern at the Capitol in Jefferson City. Her salary $200 was printed in that year's *Blue*

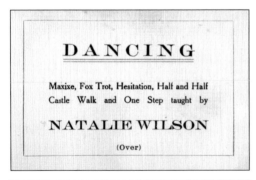

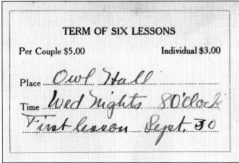

Front and back of the business card of Natalie Wilson's first business after returning from Sargent. Remember, she started hog farming several years before. The interesting thing about this card is that Nat Jr. found it—envelope addressed to him-- among her father's things while working on this book. She was unaware that they had known each other so early on.

Book, a state directory. Her friend Geneva Youngs was interning, too, though for a shorter assignment. From a very early age, Nat believed that politics were a participatory enterprise, and she took great pride in her country and great interest in the process of government.

Remember that women did not even have the right to vote yet in the United States. Passed by Congress on June 4, 1919 and ratified on August 18, 1920, the 19th amendment guarantees all American women the right to vote.

Early in the 20th Century, Warrensburg had become a very education-oriented town. There were business colleges that taught telegra-

Photo of the dapper young John Wilson, Natalie's brother and her partner in the dancing school.

Warrensburg was a very educational town. Mr. Waddell's Music School produced this version of the Mikado... Mary O. Wilson is pictured lower left. Estaline, on right, top row seated. There were schools of business, telegraphy and private lessons for the talented in many homes.

phy, shorthand, and other office skills. Art was taught in the Normal School, but teachers of voice, elocution, singing, and fine arts were also available, both in their own single teacher home studios and in upper rooms and storefronts of the downtown area, south and north of the rail line. Professor Waddell, connected to the long-running Waddell Photographic Studio, conducted a complete arts program separate from the college. His students staged a production of *The Mikado*, likely as a fundraiser, for the Elks Lodge at Magnolia Opera House, featuring Nat's sisters Mary O and Estaline.

After opening her first business, the Dancing School in Warrensburg, she took teaching jobs where she liked.

From 1915 to 1917, she took a job in a private St. Louis girl's school but found the students too spoiled and full of themselves for her taste. Natalie couldn't tolerate the way the girls had been influenced by their privileged upbringing. She then moved to teach at another Normal School, now Southeast Missouri State in Cape Girardeau.

Not yet satisfied with her educational foundation, she continued to make waves in new waters! Nat's love of swimming—informed by her knowledge of physical therapy—took precedence and she ended up in Memphis, Tennessee, and achieved a goal that was a first for women.

"WARRENSBURG GIRL NOW A LIFESAVER, *Star Journal* – April 24, 1917

> *Miss Natalie Wilson, daughter of Mr. and Mrs. John Wilson, now has the distinction of being one of the few women life savers in the United States.*
>
> *Miss Wilson is physical education director in the Misses [sic] Hutchinson's School for Girls at Memphis, Tennessee and recently took her final tests and qualified for the degree of life saver during the exhibition given at the YWCA Pool at that place, under the direction of W.E. Longfellow, lifesaving expert for the American Red Cross Society.*
>
> *Miss Wilson has been chosen to handle the physical training to be given the women this summer at Camp Wahpeton, a summer resort near Memphis where the women will be given a course of training similar to that given the men last year at Plattsburg. First aid, nursing, hospital work, military drill, swimming and lifesaving will be on the curriculum.*

FOR PROFICIENCY

This is to certify that *Miss Natalie Wilson*

of *238 South Waldran Street, Memphis, Tenn.*

has passed the test, and is entitled to be known as a

COMPETENT LIFE-SAVER

for persons of her own size in the water, having qualified as a member of the

World's Life-Saving Alliance

in the following particulars:

		Points
(A) Swimming Twenty yards in ordinary outing suit	- - -	20
(B) Disrobing in deep water and swimming eighty yards	- -	25
(C) Swimming down from surface and retrieving object in six feet of water		25
(D) Demonstrating Head, Under Arm, and Side-Stroke Rescue Methods		15
(E) Demonstrating Wrist, Front-Neck and Back-Strangle Releases	-	15
		100

And further, the recipient of this Diploma has been instructed in resuscitation of the apparently drowned by the Schaefer Method and has demonstrated it.

The tests were taken during *1917* at

the Y.M.C.A. Pool

Memphis, Tenn.

Examiner - W.E.L.

Marion H. Longfellow
Secretary

W.E. Longfellow
Chief Life-Saver

Signed by Wilbert Longfellow, this card was one of Natalie's cherished mementos. This indicates that by 1917 she was certified to train others.

Understandably proud of her accomplishments, Nat talked to James and Ginger Young, who conducted the interview that has been mentioned before. Her personal recollections:

"My folks loved to camp and I taught myself to swim when we camped down on the Niangua... They had no time to encourage me; they were too busy for that."

The Hout Natatorium, pictured here on a postcard, was opened by Walter Hout. Quite a landmark for a short time, there were numbered changing rooms which can be seen in the background of the photo. It was marketed as a Salt Water Pool.

One of the first women to receive lifesaving certification, Nat recalled that her course was taken at the Memphis YMCA, where women were not allowed. Dr. W.E. Longfellow, her instructor and the creator of the Lifesaving Movement, managed to demonstrate the ability of the intrepid young woman who had learned to swim long before in Ozark Streams by setting up a little scene. Longfellow told Nat that he would be in the pool and would ask for a volunteer to come and save him. That was her cue, she said. He was a "big, fat man who waddled like a duck" when he walked. Nat grabbed him by the head and swam for the side, "rescuing" someone much larger than herself. Then she undressed to her swimming suit while in the pool and swam four lengths. She remembered that her tennis shoes were tied too tightly, but that the exhibition ended the discussion of whether girls were up to the challenge of lifesaving.

In 1917 a new pool was built in Warrensburg near what is now the National Guard Armory on East Gay Street.

Longfellow, at Nat's encouragement, soon came to demonstrate and recruit lifeguards. The only man in his field, Longfellow organized and facilitated training of men and women for the fledgling program, now the ubiquitous Red Cross lifesaving program. *(from Young Interview recording)*

She had worn out and replaced many of the Lifesaving emblems that she had worn during her lifetime.

Amazingly, that same year she opened Camp Carry-On: Somewhere in the Ozarks. Before we get to camp, though, there are a few more feathers in the cap of this dedicated educator.

Natalie served as Head of Physical Education and Allied Sciences for the San Antonio Public Schools from 1917-1923. Supervising instruction in thirty-two Schools, she was also hired by the district to direct and stage the annual spring Parade and celebration for the

Standing at attention, left, Nat seems to have become a captain of her ambulance corps as well.

San Antonio Fiesta, which is still a tradition after a century.

The only year since 1890 that the Fiesta was not held was Nat's second year, but she found an alternative.

In 1918, Nat volunteered at Brooks Field (airfield) and at Ft. Sam Houston Hospital during the flu epidemic in San Antonio, TX . At the hospital, she met several local girls who were organizing a class in auto mechanics, training to become ambulance corps drivers overseas in World War I. She joined the class after hearing of a need for volunteers and absorbed all she was taught. She was trained as a Red Cross Ambulance Driver.

Natalie was prepared to leave for France when the war ended. "Of all the things I've done," Nat went on record as saying, "the one that I got the most out of later was my mechanical training at Ft. Sam Houston. We had to learn a lot of first aid, but we also had to learn how to take apart that old Ford motor. That was a lot of help when I returned to the farm." The war ended before her group ever shipped out, and "we were all disappointed after all that training," she said, "but we were glad the war was over."

Nat followed the British order to "Keep Calm and Carry On" through education and service. She coordinated instruction in the schools during the Academic Year and still took time to serve as a volunteer!

Captain Nat, center, with a counselor and a camper

Bagnell Dam Survey Crew, Max at right

Act II
MAKING HOMES IN THE TALL TIMBERS

Chapter Nine

DEVELOPING CAMP CARRY-ON — SOMEWHERE IN THE OZARKS

The Aims of Camp Carry-On were simple but heartfelt: In the original brochure, Nat's aims are not printed, but the camp stayed constant to this philosophy over the years, and in both of the subsequent camp booklets, these aims are printed. Clearly in the mind of the organizer, Captain Nat, these principles remained the focus.

> *Aims*
>
> The summer camp supplies a need in the character development of the growing girl which is not supplied by the home or school. Camp Carry-On seeks to make girls so happy they will share their happiness with others, to make friendships which will last through life; to develop strong and healthy bodies through activities in the open; good food and plenty of rest; to create a love of the out-of-doors; to bring about the hidden possibilities which lie within each girl, and help her to find herself.

No matter where she had traveled, Nat must have found the Ozarks the most beautiful place in the world. When she had camped there with her family as a youngster, we can hardly imagine the natural wonders that existed in little niches along the Niangua River, unspoiled by development. Ha Ha Tonka Spring and its surroundings must have seemed like a fairytale forest. If one reads the descriptions from before "The Castle" was built, the waters were so blue before the river was dammed and the cloudy water backed up into the channel that they defied description. By the late 19th Century, that particular woodland in spring and early summer already summoned up memories of the "good old days" of frontier life. So remote was the area at the time that the people who made the journey over rough and curvy dirt roads managed to escape modern times. Remember, there were no airplanes flying over, no generators making a racket, few automobile noises of any kind. Such stillness and quiet was a boon to those who found the machine age a bit jarring.

An early adopter of logos, Nat created this one which resembled the targets that the girls would be aiming for at camp.

And to Nat, who had just completed her studies under the direction of the inspiring outdoor educator Dr. Dudley Sargent, it seemed the perfect place to spend her summers "off" while continuing her teaching career in Texas. Indeed when looking back over the accomplishments of this incredible woman, one wonders how she had time for it all and whether "a day off" was ever in her thoughts.

Camp Carry-On (CCO) was established in 1917, near Old Linn Creek on the Niangua River, and was the first privately owned camp for girls west of the Mississippi. In the early days, many girls arrived in Versailles or Lebanon by train and carried their own bags, tumbling with them into the truck to travel the rest of the way to camp.

Finding land for the first camp was apparently not a problem. Near the old camping grounds of the Wilson family, Old Linn Creek seemed a perfect setting. Nat rented land for the 1917 camp from Col. R.G. Scott, who owned 5,000 acres of land around that area.

With land found, the young entrepreneur needed to find a financial backer. At the Episcopal Church, Nat had become acquainted with Mrs. Della Corum. Born in 1872, Della was the daughter of H. Strong Smith and Mary D., who lived in Grover Township in the north part of the county. In 1892 Della married John Corum of Knob Noster. They moved to Denver and were living there with their seven-year-old son Dallas in 1900. John was a telegraph operator. By 1910, Della was living in John-

Modern Dance was an element of the camp program.

son County again, with her parents, listed in the census as divorced and a milliner. As Nat put it, "She was a grass widow." From Young Interview ("Grass Widow" could mean just about anything, but it seems to mean that the man she was married to is living but not at home.)

By 1914, Della owned land in three different townships in the county, including the town of Dunksburg. It's interesting to note that Dallas's middle name, Dunkley (that of an early doctor of northeast Johnson County), signifies his family had been founders of that town. Dallas graduated from Normal #2–he is listed in the 1914 Rhetor as Fratres in Urbe with the Missouri Beta Chapter of Phi Lambda Epsilon. Also in 1914, Dallas married Mae Foster.

In 1917 Della became a founding partner in the enterprise of renting and building the original Camp Carry-On. Nat's willingness to form a partnership allowed her dream of opening the campground to become reality. Only involved at the beginning, Mrs. Corum was a true friend to the enterprising young Captain Nat.

"My mechanic training made it possible for me to keep the truck and the Model T running. I could fix the International Harvester truck in the driveway. Had to throw chains over the rear wheel drive sprocket sometimes to get through the mud. Mrs. Corum would run behind and throw the chain over that sprocket all the way up the hill. Della was there the first 5 years, before the lake came up Linn Creek. She was a card, lots of fun. Kids liked her and she had the money to get us started."

Nat remembered in the Young interview that "At first, the older girls would attend the camp, but in the later years campers were from age 10-16. I had the first private camp for girls west of the Mississippi. Camps were held in two sessions in June and July." Elma Wilson had suggested the name Camp Carry-On because of the words of encouragement that were shared among the British during World War I. In war time, when CCO first opened, the girls were taught to make flags and to communicate in semaphore code from hilltop to hilltop after hiking, as the flags were meant to be seen from a great distance. The flags caused alarm and suspicion among the locals, so that practice was modified.

The black camp cook was one of the first to break the color barrier in that area of the Ozarks, so her presence drew onlookers. One day, she went into a store and wanted to buy something and no one would wait on her. She was mad. "Can't you even sell me a hanky?" she asked. The lady left with a bandana in her hand. At that time, there was only one family of color living in Camden County.

Careful planning went into Nat's thoughts about how to best set up and record the finances of the camp. Some of her notes:

- Set up drawing account or pay yourself some set salary as manager of camp in order to meet own personal expenses.
- Set up petty cash fund on estimated account expended over some period.
- Keep separate books for store showing amounts deposited, amounts drawn and expense of store.
- Keep record of incoming tuition payments.
- Have an account at bank other than personal account if convenient.

The earliest brochure found not only describes details of requirements and activities of the camp but how the founder felt about the beauty of the location.

Camp "Folder" from 1920-In its entirety, written by Captain Nat Wilson.

Location and Equipment

Six miles from Linn Creek, Camden County, Missouri, on the Big Niangua River, is located "Camp Carry-On." It is just half way between St. Louis and Kansas City, in the south-central part of the State in the very center of the Ozarks. The best railroad points are Versailles on the north and Lebanon on the south. Campers are met at these points and brought to camp in autos, over a most beautiful country road running along the ridge of the mountains with wonderful views, over rivers and valleys and miles and miles of distance. Enough can't be said for the ideal camping spot that has been selected for "Camp Carry-On." The river of pure spring water, the big flat rock spring that supplies the drinking water, the beautiful bluff on top of which is the Camp House, the view up and down the river from here, none of these can be excelled.

The Camp House consists of two large rooms—living and dining room and kitchen. The big porches on three sides are sometimes used as classrooms and workshops. Sleeping quarters are in big 16 x 16 foot floored Army tents. Four girls to the tent. A bath house is built near the river where all bathing suits are kept. It is also used for the girls wash room.

Camp Life

Camp life is best told by a day's program, which, of course, varies day to day.

The bugle call at 6:30 a.m. 20 minutes to dress and ready for short snappy 10 minutes of "setting up" exercises. Breakfast from 7:00 – 7:30, then a half hour to make up your "bunk" and clean up in general.

It may be a hike, with a 'semaphore' lesson on the way, a first aid or home nursing lesson, target practice or military drill for an hour, folk dancing or some athletic sports. From luncheon until 2:30 we all rest and do our writing of letters for at 2:30 we do some kind of hand craft—practical art work. By that time we are all ready for a swim, the best sport of the day. After that swim and the other exercises of the day, dinner at 6:30 is one of the brightest spots of camp life. With our big living room and porches and plenty of good music, our evenings never lack for amusements. "Taps" sound at 9:30, which isn't early in camp.

The "hikes"! They are too numerous and various to describe and we have no set rule, but go where our "fancy or the call of the wild" directs. Camp "Carry-On" affords safe boats, and sometimes our "hikes" are taken by water, taking our eats along.

We can visit the famous "Ha Ha Tonka Spring" one of the most beautiful wonders of the Ozarks. And then there are the numerous float trips, one of 25 miles that brings us back within five miles of camp by land. There are many interesting spots to explore on these hikes— old mills, caves and beautiful scenery along the way. We are leaving the back of this folder for you to use in writing some friend about where you are planning to spend the summer, and should they be interested, too, we will be glad to correspond with them.

The camp season is divided into two terms—three weeks each, the first term begins July 1st. No one can enroll for less than one term. Tuition is $50 a term, including instruction, board and room, and laundry.

Camp Costume and Outfit

1 pair leggings, one-piece bathing suit and cap, 1 pair bloomers (khaki), 1 scout hat, 1 black middy tie, 2 middies (khaki), 3 pairs of shoes (2 heavy walking and 1 pair for wading), 2 sheets (small size),

one pillow and two pillowcases, bath and face towels, 1 pair of heavy blankets, one sweater, a middy suit or simple dress; Kodak, pocket knife, flashlight, and fishing tackle, etc.

Send as many things as possible by parcel post. Don't bring unnecessary clothes.

Address either of the directors for information. Miss Natalie Wilson, Graduate of Sargent's School of Physical Education; Director of Physical Education in Public Schools –San Antonio, Texas

Mrs. Delle B. Corum, Sweet Springs, Mo. (Until after July 1st), Linn Creek, Mo. (July 1-September 1)

The reasonable fee of $50 is quoted from the earliest brochure found at Camden County Historical Society. In later years as improvements were made to the camp, the tuition would be $150 for a six week session. The Mountain View Camp Carry On booklet mentions that there is a "Sister's Special and two sisters can come for $250. For additional fees girls could participate in horseback riding (10 hours for $15 or 25 hours for $30}."

Each morning, Captain Nat blew the bugle call that charmed the campers out of their slumbers and into yet another exciting and eventful day in the wooded hills and streams.

A special nearby cave, still a natural feature, offered the excitement of adventures in spelunking and wall scaling. From 1917–1930, the Carry-On Girls explored the exquisite beauty of Bridal Cave near the camp. It was not yet developed as a tourist attraction, so Captain Nat only had to ask her friend, Col. Scott, for permission to enter. Spectacular stalactites and stalagmites were seen by candlelight, torchlight, and later flashlights. At the end of the main path was a dead end with a crawl space twelve feet up the wall. Big Nat was an advocate of "wall scaling" so up and over the girls went to see a big crystal clear blue-green lake. The area was eventually excavated, so tourists could walk to the edge of the lake. Since opening to tourists in 1948, over 2,900 weddings have taken place there.

Star Journal – June 5, 1919, "Home from San Antonio," "Miss Natalie Wilson, superintendent of physical instruction in the public schools of San Antonio, and Miss Geneva Youngs, teacher of music and drawing in the Junior High School of the same city, arrived home

Saturday. These young ladies were both reelected in their positions for the coming year, which is the best evidence that their work was satisfactory. Miss Gladys Anderson, who was superintendent of drawing, has not arrived home yet, but she, too, has her position for the coming year."

Estaline and Nat Wilson at camp... Loving sisters.

Misses Natalie Wilson and Geneva Youngs had returned to Missouri from their teaching positions, and Gladys Anderson, though on a different timetable, was following a similar path. Their admirable positions in Texas had been hard won, as new doors were opening for women in leadership, and these friends were already experienced educators whose mission did not end when the doors of their respective schools closed in May. Captain Nat, the young entrepreneur, noticed that her talents and vision blended nicely with that of other young women from her hometown. Physical education, music, the arts, and outdoor experiences would be a solid educational foundation for a camp like the one she had experienced in New Hampshire. Her friends would be mainstays of the staff for her camp in the early days.

By 1925, Nat had enlisted the help of her family. A *Star Journal* article from June 1925 states:

"Camp Carry-On Opens Wednesday—Miss Natalie Wilson opens her annual Camp Carry-On near Linn Creek Wednesday. Miss Natalie has been at the camp for several days making the opening arrangements. Her mother, Mrs. J.H. Wilson, and Sisters Misses Estaline and Olive left in their car Saturday morning to spend a part of the summer at camp."

In December of 1925, Nat was invited by Jesse F. Williams of the Physical Education Department of the Teachers College at Columbia University in New York City to become a part-time instructor, with full-time possibilities. She would be "teaching a combination of different courses, – Social Dancing, some gymnastics, and a new course that I am calling Daily Physical Activities... Let me know if you are free as soon as you can." This job was declined because Nat's summers were already full of activity.

Chapter Ten

MAX: WWI BOOT CAMP AND THE AMERICAN EXPEDITIONARY FORCE

Three Letters of Recommendation for Officer's Training, dated July 11, 1917

From August Ahrens, professor of Industrial Arts, State Normal School, Warrensburg

To whom it may concern: The bearer of this, Mr. Max Prussing, of Warrensburg, Missouri, is a young man of sterling character and personal worth. During the past four years that I have known him I have had every reason to put full confidence in him. He is strong of mind and body and has no bad habits. All of these qualities fit him for the office for which he hopes to train. I commend Mr. Prussing to you.

Several friends, and a rare view of the Normal #2 athletic logo, ca 1916

Max and his friends on the move, preparing stealth tactics for World War I service?

From W.J. Mayes, Mayor of the City of Warrensburg

Dear Sir: It gives me pleasure to commend to you Mr. Max M. Prussing of this city, for your most favorable consideration, as an applicant for reenlistment in the Officers Reserve Corp. I have known Mr. Prussing for many years. He stands high as a young man in this community. His habits are par excellent, character excellent, and he is a bright, active young man, and in my earnest judgement would prove a good officer.

From J.D. Eads, Cashier People's National Bank of Warrensburg

Dear Sir: I have known the bearer of this letter, Mr. Max M. Prussing of Warrensburg, Mo., since his childhood. He is a young man of exemplary habits and character and deserves the respect and confidence of everyone. I commend him for your most favorable consideration for enlistment in the Officers Reserve Corps.

Max Prussing ventured out on his own journey, leaving Warrensburg to serve in World War I. Before leaving for Oklahoma, Max applied and was accepted for officer training. He moved to Independence, Missouri. Max rented a room in a house next door to the Wallace Family where future First Lady Bess Wallace still lived with her parents. With her beau, Harry S. Truman, she attended the dance socials for officers and trainees. On several occasions, Harry asked, "Max, would you walk Bess home for me?" And he did. Max's memory was always the same, "I liked Bess better than Harry!" He left Independence, Missouri, on September 26, 1917, and the correspondence that remains is a good illustration of the intellect and character of the man Max Prussing.

The letters begin soon after Max left for boot camp and continued all through the war. People today forget that correspondence was not always "immediate." These letters would first be posted stateside, but later after Max was stationed in the European Theater, the letters would take a long time to arrive, first being censored by the proper authorities so that locations and strategies of the U.S. Armed Forces would not be compromised by homesick soldiers. Throughout the letters, it is clear that Max misses his family but would not have missed the Army experience even to be with them. He asks after a girl Ruth, and admires his sisters for continuing their education. Almost every letter mentions the farm and wishing he could help his father. Information about other local "boys" is exchanged, and the health of all asked after. Socks and different weights of underwear and clothing are discussed

---

Important Dates & Whereabouts of Sgt. Max Prussing during WWI

- Entered military service- Aug 5, 1917
- Left Independence for Camp Doniphan, OK- September 26
- Arrived Camp Doniphan- September 28
- Arrived Camp Mills, Long Island, NY- May 14, 1918
- Left Camp Mills for New York- May 18
- Sailed overseas onboard the S.S. Saxon- May 19
- Arrived Liverpool England- May 31
- Rest Camp at Romsey, England- June 1
- Sailed from South Hampton- June 6
- LeHarve- June 7 & 8
- Angiers- June 9
- Billeted- June 9
- Arrived Coetquidan- July 9
- Vosges Mountains- August 20
- Argonne Forest Sept 26- Oct. 7
- In position near Verdun- Oct 7
- Drive north of Verdun- Nov. 9
- Armistice signed- November 11
- Left Verdun on furlough- Dec. 1
- Returned to duty- Dec. 19
- Left Camp LaBeholle- Jan. 22, 1919
- Arrived Rosiers- Jan. 23
- Passed in troops review for Gen Pershing, Commercy- Feb. 27
- Left Rosiers- March 6
- Arrived Courcement- March 9 Left- March 29
- Arrived Brest- March 31
- Embarked for home from Brest, on German Liner Zeppelin April 9, 1919.

frequently until the 129th Field Artillery ships out for France. After that, the Army takes care of and completely occupies the attentions of "its own" until the Armistice.

Excerpts from his Letters:

September 28, 1917. Arrived at Camp Doniphan, Fort Sill, Lawton, OK

October 9—Thot I would write you while I have the time. We are busy all day long and so have to write at night by candlelight. We have

Tents at Camp Doniphan where Max spent his first months in the U.S. Army, the camp covered 2000 acres of land

Field Artillery drills at Camp Doniphan stretched over the Oklahoma landscape

In a more sober pose, these young men are going to the European Front. (Max, left) At times the dust and silt three inches deep would greet the recruits when they returned from training

Back home, Max's sister Louise also knows how to handle a gun, but Max sends some advice home

a fine time here. There are four of us from Warrensburg in the same tent and Ben (Grover) comes up about every night with a paper from home and we discuss the news. I am still working with horses and am breaking and training the Officer's horses now. We have a bunch of good horses, but they are all wild. They came from Reno, Nevada and were all plains horses, most of them never having been ridden. [Max also asks his folks to send his "light weight woolen Union suit I bought last spring"] The grub is good, whenever it gets bad the boys just wreck the mess hall and beat up the cooks. Tell everyone hi for me, I cannot write them all.

November 7—It is sure some sight when the whole regiment is mounted and starts out together, makes a string over two miles long. I have been promoted again to a higher non-commissioned officer and am drawing $36.00 a month. They are very slow paying us. . . .Sam Baston, the boy who used to deliver the Star at home has the paper business in this whole camp. I see him twice every day when he stops at our tent. He sure was glad to see this Warrensburg bunch. If you will give me Mr. R.P. Owens address I will try and look him up. You see there are about 40,000 men here now and they are spread out over a piece of ground 20 x 15 MILES, so you see it is a hard job to find any-one.... I have gained 10 pounds in weight, so you know we are getting plenty to eat.

November 19—This 35 division stands a pretty good chance of go-ing to France this winter and I would rather make that trip than have any commission and all these new commissioned men will never see service outside of the U.S. There is also every chance for advancement here in the artillery and at that a non com's job is pretty soft. Must close now, Yours, Max

November 23—Dear Mother, I received your letter this evening and am answering it tonight. I have decided to go to the next training camp and have put in my application. The captain says I stand a very good chance and from the looks of the other applicants I do not think I will have much trouble.

I am glad to hear that Stanley Demand is coming home and hope that he has a good commission. There is not much good about a com-mission, excepting the pay, for you get the dirty end of every thing and have to work all the time including Sunday.... Must close now, Max.... Do not worry about me going to France for I am going if I get the chance.

December 30—[Looking out for his little sister Louise Prussing] Tell Louise to cut out that writing to fellows who put their names in the pa-per. If she could see the specimens she is writing to, she'd cut it out. Boys who put their names in the paper are the roughnecks of the camp or they would not be doing such stunts. I have obtained and burned the letters she wrote and the boys are now in the guard house with charges filed against them for it is against regulations to do such. So tell her to cut it out, and see that she does it!

January 5, 1918—Well, I have moved again and am now attending the Divisional Training School which started yesterday. . . . Three men were sent from each Battery and I happened to be one. . . . I will miss the mounted drill that we have here, for it will be foot drill from now on.

January 26—We have been doing infantry drill for three weeks and have been working and hiking all the time.... We have been in bar-racks for over two weeks but give me the tents for mine—they are not so crowded and are more comfortable.

February 2—We start drilling at eight in the morning and drill un-til 9:30 then have a class until noon. After noon we march across the horseshoe and ride for three hours or "equitation" as it is called, then we have a class in the operation of the range finder and Battery Commander's telescope (used to find range and angles for firing).

I would be glad to receive any of the daily papers you might care to send. When Ben Grover was here I used to read his papers, daily.

Feb 14—Tell dad there is no need for banking that money that is sent home, but to take it and use it for I do not want it and he might as well have the use of it, that much money will help to pay Charlie

Charlie Goodwin in the door of the Prussing Barn

Goodwin's wages...or tell him to hire another worker for I know that he and Charlie can hardly keep up…. Now make him use that money for if it is not in use you might as well have a lot of rocks piled up in the bank…. I have finished the Army school of horsemanship and now have the degree of expert horseman. Have entered another school for experts under French army instructors, a school of what is called "High Schooled Horsemanship". One of the instructors, a French Major, cannot speak English but believe me he is some fancy rider.

I have learned more since I joined the Army than I ever did at any school or under any instructor. In the army one learns to think and act in one movement and believe me it sure does develop the mind and the muscles…

March 2—Our Battery at the training school was broken up, not caring to be in the infantry I resigned from the school along with all the rest of the artillerymen who were to be sent to the infantry. I would rather be a sergeant in the Artillery than a Captain in the Infantry.

I am now an instructor in Equitation and have a fine job.

March 15, 1918—I have been very busy this week; have been acting as Stable Sergeant this week while the other Sgt. was on furlough. Taking care of 165 horses is no small job for one man. This battalion has been firing every other day and I have had charge of one of the gun sections…. I am sure glad I left the officer's school and came back here for we are doing some real soldiering here. Most of the artillerymen were transferred to the infantry and then came back to their regiments. I have found that these three month officers absolutely are not efficient and no one respects them in this camp, "pinch hitters" they are called.

The Battalion is giving a big dance and supper in Lawton tomorrow night and I think I shall go. We have rented a dance hall and café for the occasion. We are going to get forty more drafted men from Funston here to fill the Batt. I guess it will be my job to instruct them in equitation, that means several months hard work for me. I am glad to hear that Stanley likes the French people. I do not think we will ever get over there, not for many months at least. Send candy whenever you like…or have time to make it. Must close now and go to school.…
Yours, Max

March 23, 1918—I wish dad could see the horses we have in this regiment. E. Bat. has all sorrel and chestnut horses any of them would bring from $150-$200 on the market, all these horses are perfect with not a blemish on them.

I have a horse for a mount that is as near like old Ginger as can be and with more life. This horse has out run every horse in camp and also cleared that bar in a jumping contest at 5 feet two inches. I have also ridden this horse in fancy riding contests bare back and he always wins. Each Bat. has a team and every two weeks we have riding contests. Myself and an Indian pardner of mine named Lone Star have won three contests so far and will probably represent the regiment in regimental contests. Must close now, Yours Max.

March 28—Dear Folks, We have been out at the pistol range all day, went out early this morning and went into camp. The dust was blowing so thick it was nearly impossible to see a target at 25 yards and as a result some very poor shooting was done…

I have been in the saddle for about two weeks straight and have nearly forgotten how to walk.

Say you had better send my last allotment down here. We have to buy a lot of small articles such as toilet articles and some clothing for overseas service. They are very slow about getting us clothing. I have had only one pair of pants for three months and bought them myself. The last bunch of clothing we got was all undersize stuff and none of it would fit me… I cannot come home unless we stay here for several months more as they have stopped all furloughs until April 15

April 11—I am glad I quit the [Officer] training school when I did. Only eighty were given commissions and nearly fifty have been asked to resign already. A man has to know something to be an Artillery officer and it cannot be done in three months. You might as well give up the idea of me coming home on furlough for it can hardly be did. [He appears to have made it though, as the next letter reports the trip home nearly broke him and that he will need another allotment payment forwarded from home.]

April 25—Back in camp…. Mr. Stone will send photographs on. One of the girls can stop in and get them (at his studio). They are already paid for.

[No matter where he went or what officer encouraged him to try another posting, Max chose to stay right where he wanted to be, where he started, and was most adept, with the horses and artillery guns. All this while at Camp Doniphan, where Harry Truman was running a canteen.]

May 7—Dear Folks, Well we are leaving here at last, this afternoon we received orders to prepare to leave within 36 hours and we have been working hard ever since. First the horses' shoes had to be pulled and the horses turned in to the remount, then all harness and equipment packed and loaded so we will get no more sleep for a few nights.

Do not write to me until I give you my next address for we will be on the way by the time this letter reaches you. I do not know where we are going but I am glad to be moving for it is getting hot down here. Must close now and get to work. I sent my locker home today by express… C.O.D. [cash on delivery means that the receiver must pay the postage] Yours, Max

May 11—now in Indiana … riding in tourist Pullmans and are well fixed [in Pullman cars on a train, there were attendants to care for your needs and make your bed, etc.] meals on the train are excellent … in high spirits … enjoying the ride. Twelve trainloads of artillery are on the move. Will stop at Camp Mills in Long Island before going across. Tell "Doc" Rundell and Mr. Beazell that I am on my way over.

May 14—Camp Mills, Long Island. Saw the Statue of Liberty and many passenger and battleships on the way. About 100,000 men here now, [and this] is not such a healthy camp nor as good a location as Doniphan. Write me soon as you receive this letter and I may receive your reply before we leave here.

On May 19th, 1918 Max shipped out for the European Theater on the S.S. Saxon.

Letter from June 6, 1918, Soldier's Mail, Southampton, England

Do not worry at all about me for I am in the habit of getting along allright wherever I am and you know army life agrees with me. Will write again soon.

Sgt M. Prussing, Bat. E. 129th F.A., American Expeditionary Forces via N.Y. Censored Lt. F. M. Feuner

June 17, 1918—Censored by Lt. Dyer Bty E 129FA

Further from home… through traveling for a while. Billeted in small country village in Central France all over the country in old barns, burnt and vacant houses. Our quarters are good in a couple of old bowling alleys in the center of village. French are cordial and hospitable…. We are far from "Sam's Country." Food now very good for we are back on our own army rations. English ration seemed very small to us. The English are not such great eaters … and thought us hogs.

June 22—We are now permitted to tell a few of the more important places on our route over. Landed at Liverpool made a night trip into Romsey England a rest camp, next to South Hampton and then to La Harve France, through to Algiers and are now quartered some distance from there. I like the French people though not much conversation. Weather is nice and cool and it does not get dark until after 10 o'clock so we have no use for lights of any kind.

June 25—There is nothing much of importance in my locker. I forgot to send the key, but open if you wish. Be sure to keep everything of mine in shape. Have Louise go over my guns once every week or so and not let them rust. Glad to hear of girls' graduation, I suppose they will be teaching before long. Tell Rundell and Beazell I should like to hear from them. I am glad father is dealing in good horses once more. I was beginning to think he had given them up.

July 3—Our quarters are excellent, large stone buildings. The sergeants have a mess [hall] and club room where nights are spent with plenty of music and entertainments…. I am going to school every afternoon and guess I will be as long as the war lasts. Write often and tell me all the news of home and friends.

July 7—I have not heard from you in some time. I have been putting in full time every day during the week. Was on a horse today for the first time since leaving Doniphan. Am so fat I can hardly ride at all, but riding takes it off…. These French peoples ways seem strange to an American. Try working one horse to a two wheeled wagon and haul large loads of hay as we do with two horses. They never seem to stop for Sunday but go right ahead. Write me all the news at home as we never see papers over here.

n.d.—in the week since I have written have been on the move continuously both day and night. It rains every day, however the ground does not become muddy. At present I am acting stable sergeant, some very good horses, but not as good as we had in the states.

July 28—am still in charge of the stables, a job which has no end and knows no holidays. Not much news.

September 7—I expect you have been doing a lot of needless worrying. I have not been where I could secure writing material or mail a letter. Never close to any town until now. Quartered in a large stone barn, first roof in more than a month. Just returned from the front where we did some work against "Fritz." Several days ago I saw some of the Warrensburg boys I knew, among them George Thrailkill, Luther Anderson and Pap Stilwell, all were in good health. I have now received all your letters to date. I wish you had some of this rain, but am glad you do not have to sleep out in it or on the ground, to boot.

Another thing I almost forgot, I had a bath and a complete change of clothing yesterday, the first in two months. I felt very much like a different person. In the best of health … do not worry about me.

We have been fed exceptionally well considering the circumstances under which we have been working, our rolling kitchen travels right along with us and always serves the meals.

I am in the best of health so do not worry about me. Max

n.d. – Enclosed—X-mas package coupon, I am mailing a little late, but think it will reach you in time. This is what I wish to have you send me. One pair of those big heavy leather mittens with sheep skin lining as I used to wear at home. One dozen MIKADO No. 2 Lead Pencils from Mr. Beazell. Fill the rest of the box with Hershey's Chocolate bars. These things are not obtainable over here. I have all the good heavy woolen underwear I can carry, also more bug heavy socks than I know what to do with…. It is not cold, just rains everyday… disagreeable. Sorry to hear of Stanley [Demand] being wounded. I have been scratched up several times but not hurt.

I received a letter from John Rowland … also one from Stanley. Stan has recovered from his wound and probably in active service by this

Early in September of 1918, the 129th Field Artillery undertook one of the longest and most brutal road marches of the War from the Vosges Mountains to the Argonne Forest. The men guided their horses and equipment over a hundred miles of crowded, muddy back roads to the new American Sector. Then it was on to Verdun. Max served in Battery E of the 129th, while Captain Harry Truman was with Battery D.

time. John has been in the hospital at Quantico Virginia for some time and expects to come over very soon. Eugene Sollars returned this week after a six week stay in hospital. I will be receiving $15 more in allotment for the duration of the war. Tell dad to put it where it will do the most good. Am sending you some French currency. A franc and a half... worth about two bits [25 cents]

[The Armistice which officially ended World War I was signed on November 11, 1918.]

November 19—I received your letter today telling me of Gail Carmack's death. Certainly very sorry to hear...papers say a great many dying of influenza at home, it was hard for me to believe them. Not affected us here so far. You say you have not heard for 6 weeks, well those were busy times and it was impossible for me to write but now since the armistice has been agreed upon I will have more time and will write more often. I do not think that Charlie [a black gentleman who worked for Max's father] will be called in the draft and am glad of it for I know how much dad needs him. Our Warrensburg crowd is still together in this regiment and exchange news from home. Last time I saw George Thrailkill was in the Argonne drive, I suppose he is still with the doughboys.

I had a birthday last week and knew nothing about it until that night when I happened to be doing a bit of thinking while lying in my dugout. It was also the first night that no shells had been coming our way for a long time. These are the quietest days in France for many long years.

Verdun, Nov. 23—Sunday morning, beautiful, ground frozen enough to keep from being muddy. Breakfast this morning was hotcakes, butter and syrup, steak, gravy, butter bread and coffee—what more could a man ask for? It seems funny to have a roof over one's head again instead of a pup tent or wet dug out. I must stop and sew the buttons on my clothes.

Dec. 8—American Y.M.C.A., on furlough since Nov. 28 and now at a once famous resort in southern France, Le Mont Dore, just north of the Alps.... this is the first place I have seen a Y.M.C.A. since I left the military training school 5 months ago...

You see we were on the front for over 3 months, when we were relieved at one place we went to another and were always under shell fire. I hope everything is alright at the farm. I hope to be back next summer in time to help some. Max P.

Christmas Day 1918

The second Christmas I have spent in the Army. Excellent dinner today. At camp, outside Verdun the mud is just knee deep, we have been here nearly 2 months and it has rained every day. One day the sun shone for about an hour. On twenty days furlough, I visited some of the larger cities of France.

It seems you have not heard from me for some time. I think there were about two months when I had no chance to write. We went on to the Vosages mountains about the middle of August then came to the Argonne front and stayed with that big drive for several weeks. I expect you have read about the battle of the Argonne forest, supposed to have been one of the hardest fought battles over here.... the doughboys deserve a lot of credit.... From the 9th to the 11th of Nov. we were not

Remnants of the war, dog tags, sergeant's stripes and a sewing kit to repair his own uniform, as mentioned in the letters

a thousand yards from Fritz. We heard about the signing of the Armistice about ten in the morning and believe me that last hour was a hot one for the Dutch. We fired right up until the last minute and were right in plain view on a hill sending it to the dutch machine guns. At 11 o'clock the firing ceased and the French started singing the Marseilles and every American joined in and then they sang the Star Spangled Banner and the Germans started singing too, I guess the poor devils were glad it was over.

For three months we were on the front or were within hearing distance. All travel was done over land and at night, believe me that is hard on a man, especially with very little to eat.

Did you ever read an article in the *K.C. Star* by O.P. Higgins titled, "In Battle with the 129 F.A."? In this article he speaks of "Bat. A of Independence" which was a misprint and was really Bat. E. He also speaks of a craps game by a gun crew beside one of the pieces. This reporter—Higgins–stayed with us for several days and was much amused by the boys and their indifference to shell fire. The paper was an October number, one of the boys here received the clipping from home about a month ago. The boys from Independence received word yesterday of the death their Sgt. Bowles from a shrapnel wound so that dampened our Christmas… he was well liked by everyone.

I go on guard in a few minutes most of the boys are drunk and have not finished celebrating so I will have to take care of my share of them until they go to sleep. I hope to spend the 4th of July somewhere in the U.S.

December 29—And still it rains…. I used to hear people talk about sunny France, they surely were never in this part of France. Hip boots and rain coats are worn continually or a person would never be dry…. [W]e have become accustomed by now and the sun would probably hurt our eyes.

We are now using mules in place of horses for artillery work. They seem much more satisfactory and are able to do more work and get along on a lot less feed. It seems funny to see six mules going down the road pulling guns and caissons.

The French horses did not amount to much for artillery work, they could not stand the long night marches when we got only two or three hours rest. Believe me that was real war… For three weeks we hiked every night and I learned to sleep in a saddle as well as I used to in my own bed at home. The nights are very long. It is dark at 4 o'clock and is not light until after 8 in the morning… very few amusements so the evenings are spent playing cards, washing and mending clothes. The weather is warm for this time of year…. p.s. took a bath today, the first in a month or so—I forget when. Have just finished boiling out some clothes to kill a few cooties and other live stock. I feel looonesome without my cooties. [for the modern day reader—cooties means lice, a common affliction of the soldiers]

Experienced in the field and having lost quite a lot of weight wagon/artillery soldiers have an opportunity to wash their uniforms on a washboard at a trough of water. Max takes a moment to sit, but not to rest

Verdun, Jan 6, 1919—Am still here in the mud hole and see no chance of getting away soon…. I do not know what it would be like to see the sun shine once more. It has rained every day since we have been here. We are not troubled by "the flu" here in spite of the mud and rain. This has been the warmest winter I have ever passed it has not frozen the garden vegetables as yet. The French soldiers always have gardens around their camps and they are still eating fresh cabbage.

January 19—[more talk of baths and lice] Some of the boys are anxious to go home, but I would like a trip into Germany first.

So far I have seen the most of France, some of Switzerland and Italy and would like to see more for this will probably be my only trip on this side of the pond. There is to be an American Expeditionary Force Horse Show sometime this spring. We have entered a 6 mule team and I have entered a saddle horse and also in the fancy and trick riding, anything to pass the time

A scene drawn by a war correspondent made it into a Kansas City paper mentioning the 129th Field Artillery, a Kansas City unit

February 8—It has been some time since I have written to you but I have been very busy. Spent a week in a field hospital with a bad foot caused by wearing rubber boots for three months… met several fellows whom I had known at the Normal.

February 14—I have rented a room with a French family and am very comfortably situated. I do not see how these people live, they are dirty as the dickens. Their houses and barns are all in the same building and all buildings join one another. The living rooms are usually in the back end of a barn and have never a bit of sunlight in them. I have sent several souvenir shell cases home but do not know whether you will ever get them or not—there are so many mail clerks between France and Mo. There is a trinket or two inside these cases. The shells were all fired by this Bat. Upon several different fronts…

Tell dad he should have plenty of mules and horses on hand for that farm has to start producing on a larger scale when I get back. I have been living with horses and mules ever since I have been in the Army and have learned a lot from the army veterinary schools so I do not think I would be able to live without them. A stable sgt. In the army has to know every one of 165 horses, has to know what team the horse works in and its driver. One soon becomes lonesome without the horses. At present there are only rumors of this division returning … but I hope to be home in time for harvest.

These souvenirs of Verdun and the Argonne were carefully crafted by local artisans from spent 75 mm. brass shells from Max's gun. A precious gift, sent home by army mail, they stand about 10' high

February 20—Dear Folks, There is nothing much to write. Monday we were inspected and reviewed by General Pershing. The 35th Division passed a good inspection and were very highly praised by the Commander in Chief. The Gen. is a fine looking old man and one cannot help but admire him the first time you see him.

Feb 25—Ward Johnson was in to Bar-Le-Duc a day or so ago and saw Kenneth Robinson and Otto Heberling… from them Ward was able to find out quite a bit of news from home. Doc Powers is now a captain, that old hot air of his must have gotten him by.

April 20—Postcard, Soldier's Mail, Port of New York—Arrived Safely Today. Going to Camp Mills Long Island. Will write letter soon. Sgt. Max Prussing

[According to Natalie Jr., of the battalions in the 129th, Max's "E" Battery was the only one to use mules, in addition to horses, and was the most successful in getting the cannons and equipment through the notorious deep mud of that war. Of the 300,000 mules sent overseas for the war effort, none returned. They were either killed in action or eaten by hungry survivors whose situations had suffered because of the war. Eight million horses, donkeys, and mules died during World War I (Aug 4, 2014 Horsetalk.co.nz).]

April 22, 1919—Hempstead, N.Y. Camp Mills, Long Island
Dear Folks

No doubt you are greatly surprised to hear from me, this is the first letter I have written since we were way over in Eastern France, we have been on the move for a long time. I suppose the Kansas City paper has kept you well posted concerning our movements. There is always a reporter with us. We sailed from Brest on April 9 aboard the German ship Zeppelin and landed at Hoboken, N.J. on April 20. It was Easter Sunday morning, we came into the harbor shortly after daylight and docked at 9 o'clock. We were given a great welcome by the people of New York City, were well fed, had the first piece of pie and cake for one year.

We were taken directly to Camp Mills. Have not been doing much the last few days, we were given new clothes and everyone looks much better now.

I spent twenty-four hours in New York city, went to Winter Garden Theatre and saw the Midnight Frolics, sure is some Large town, I intend to go to Newark, N.J. and Hoboken tomorrow.

I mailed, or rather sent a package home by express this afternoon, so go to the express office and get it for me and be sure and keep the contents, especially my old "side partner," for I carried him a long time.

The regiment will be split up here and sent to Camp Funston for discharge, do not come to Kansas City with the expectation of seeing a parade for there will be none. About half the men in this regiment are from K.C., the rest are from Texas, Alabama, and Georgia and will be sent to their respective states for discharge. Expect to be here about a week. Will probably be three weeks before I get home. Yours, Max

From Kansas City newspaper articles about the 129th Field Artillery in WWI — no dates

Hard to Move the Guns — Artillery in Argonne Forest Had Heavy Going—Lieutenant C.C. Bundschu Tells Auxiliary Members—Gas Attack also Hampered Men Behind the Guns

How the 129th Field Artillery leaving the road to the heavier guns, went across country in its effort to keep up with the infantry of the 35th Division

The first day we gave the infantry a strong creeping barrage, but the second and third days our fire was interrupted by the changes of position we had to make. The infantry advanced rapidly and we kept after them the best we could over trench systems, wire entanglements and shell holes. I have seen as many as thirty cannoneers pulling on ropes attached to a gun and struggling at the wheels in an attempt to help the exhausted horses pull it out of a mud hole. We were doing all that men could do.

Wiped Out a Nest

On November 5th the 35th Division was taken out of the line to fill up with replacements, the 81st Division making the relief. The 60th F.A. Brigade, of which the 129th F.A. is a part, remained in support, however. On one occasion [Max's] Battery "E" of the 129th under Lt. Harry Sturgis of Independence, MO, was ordered forward to knock out a machine gun, holding up the infantry. The section went into action at a range of nine hundred meters with direct fire and accomplished its mission without a casualty. The doughboys of the 81st would say they expected us any minute to fasten bayonets to the muzzles of the 75s and go over the top with them.

When the furlough finally came through, Max was treated to some luxury at a resort in the French Alps

A Letter from Capt. John H. Thacher, adjutant of the 129th Field Artillery, appeared in a Kansas City paper, detailing the treatment of the Soldiers in France after the war ended. It was titled Furloughs are Frolics:

"I am down here with some twelve hundred lively young pleasure seekers who are having a 7 day leave in one of the United States Army leave areas of which you have heard so much. Rather than have the young American soldier person wander at large over the broad realm of France on his furlough, or rather to prevent his immediate gravitation to Paris, these various leave centers are established. They are generally at or near some popular summer resort of healthful and attractive surroundings, where there is enough to do and not too many unwholesome experiments to be tried. The young man who has been under shell fire, possessed with a colony of active and educated cooties, fed up on corned willie [corned beef] and beans, and bored with the mud and rain and tedium of life in dugouts and rough shacks in the Verdun forests is suddenly caught up following one of the strange incantations of military necromancy, pounced upon, and violently 'de-loused' dressed in new blouse and overcoat, hustled aboard a truck and taken down to the old shell torn ruins of the Verdun Rail Station; there kept waiting for thirty-six hours while various Olympic powers debate the subject of his transportation and car equipment for the journey, loaded on one train, then taken off again, then finally loaded on the palatial 'side door Pullman' (boxcar).

It takes three days in the boxcar, where neither sitting or standing is a good option, to reach the destination. Two day rations of food did not last the journey, and when the tired and hungry soldiers finally leaving the train to find 'a veritable happy hunting ground.' A Paradise on Earth. He wakes in a few hours in a clean, soft, well flaxed bed, in a white room of a first class hotel.... He dresses in a daze, goes down to a sunny dining room and eats off clean linen and china and rejoices prayerfully in plenty of shirred eggs. Eggs, for which he has violently struggled as a rare treat at every half demolished town he has passed through on his long hikes of the last three months. Then he strolls off to new delights. There are hot mineral baths; a great Casino—the former gambling pavilion of the place magnificent in design and appointments, with sunrooms, music rooms, theatres, movies, libraries, writing rooms, cafes, dancing halls, all run in princely fashion by the Y.M.C.A.

He is his own master.... he returns in a daze to a 6 course table dinner ("and you don't have to wash the plates, captain, just leave them dirty and they furnish more!.")"

The 129th Field Artillery Returns to Kansas City

The Missouri spirit is evident in the attitude of the folk awaiting the return of their beloved soldiers after their long absence overseas. "The delayed arrival of the 129th Field Artillery until tomorrow morning will mean a bigger and better homecoming celebration. The women's committee will have more time in which to get the chicken and strawberries ready, the bands will be better tuned and the whistles set up to make more noise. The mayor's committee expects to make the welcome to the artillery men tomorrow the noisiest the city ever has thrown. Two trainloads of servicemen were transported by the Chicago and Alton Railway, the first at 5:30 a.m. and the rest in time for the 9:30 a.m. parade.

Max returns to Kansas City with 129th Field Artillery

The victorious soldiers returned to Kansas City to great fanfare marching through a beautiful, if temporary Arc de Triomphe on the way to Convention Hall. Max's cousin Ruth Wiloughby told Natalie Jr. that Ruth remembered her father holding her up high to watch Max marching by.

Max kept a copy of this poem among other mementos from his time in WWI.

In Flanders Fields
by Lieutenant Colonel John McCrae

The World's Most Famous WAR MEMORIAL POEM Composed at the battlefront on May 3, 1915, during the second battle of Ypres, Belgium:

In Flanders fields the poppies blow
Between the crosses, row on row,
That mark our place; and in the sky
The larks, still bravely singing, fly
Scarce heard amid the guns below.
We are the Dead. Short days ago
We lived, felt dawn, saw sunset glow,
Loved and were loved, and now we lie
In Flanders fields.

Take up our quarrel with the foe:
To you from failing hands, we throw
The torch; be yours to hold it high.
If ye break faith with us who die
We shall not sleep, though poppies grow
In Flanders fields.

Chapter Eleven

A Teaching Career Means Continuing Education

Continuing education for teachers has been the way to increase pay and advance into administrative roles since the beginning of formal teacher training. Nat, exposed to the "Normal School" system since a child and with older sisters who were progressing in their own careers, had a full understanding of how that hierarchy worked. Immediately upon beginning to teach in San Antonio, Texas, she had moved into an administrative position. Upon leaving San Antonio, Nat took a temporary position to fill in for an absent instructor at Central Missouri State Teachers College (UCM) in 1923.

Never one to rest on her laurels, Nat aspired to continue her education at the only place available to women to get post graduate training and certification. It appears that Nat spent much of the 1924-25 academic year in New York City at Columbia University Teachers College.

From their catalog:

The policy of Teachers College is to adapt its work to the needs of advanced students, who have chosen Education as a professional career. It follows therefore, that the requirements for admission emphasize maturity, experience in teaching or equivalent professional service and academic scholarship appropriate to the subject or field in which the student intends to specialize. The actual requirements vary according to the previous training of the student and the needs of professional leadership in each particular field, some positions demanding exceptional technical skill, while others stress scholarly attainment. It is the aim of Teachers College to suit both the requirements for admission and for graduation to the actual conditions which prevail in American education.

The normal requirement for the degree of Bachelor of Science of students who present two years of an approved curriculum completed elsewhere is two years of prescribed and elective courses.

The prescribed courses are as follows a) A major course or program in the particular subject in which the candidate elects to specialize; b) Courses amounting to 16 points in English, history and the natural sciences; c) Courses amounting to twelve points in the history and philosophy of Education and Educational Psychology.

Students who offer more than the minimum requirement for admission may be given advanced standing and substitution may be allowed for any prescribed course that has been complete elsewhere, but every candidate for a degree must spend in residence one academic year or two half years.

Though no record remains of the actual courses taken, those available to Captain Nat included:

- Courses for Supervisors of Scouting and Recreational Leadership
- Personal and School Hygiene (a new and growing science that also included stopping the spread of contagious diseases).
- Physical Education courses included: Anatomy, Gymnastics, Folk and Clog Dancing, Natural Gymnastics, Swimming, Music in Physical Education, and Games. There were courses in First Aid and in leading extra-curricular programs. Anthropometry (measuring of different human characteristics) was continued from her previous work at Sargent.

Natalie earned degrees from Columbia University, NYC. Two diplomas were given in October of 1925. Stating that "Natalie Wilson has satisfactorily completed a course of study leading to an academic degree and has demonstrated professional ability as a Teacher of Hygiene and Physical Education". A separate diploma was conferred for "Bachelor of Science with all the rights, privileges and immunities thereunto". —October 28, 1925

The particular courses that Nat took are lost to time, but the above excerpts from a contemporary course catalog offer some clues about her exposure to up-to-date practices. Research for this work included searching Columbia University course announcements, Alumni Federation Cards, and Biographical Data Historical, all that is available for research from the University Archives. At the time she attended Columbia, some well-known educators were on staff, including John Dewey (of Dewey Decimal system fame), who was Professor of Philosophy in the Teachers College.

Nat continued her philosophy "if life gives you lemons, make lemonade." Playing basketball while attending Columbia, Nat suffered a badly broken ankle. The doctor told her it was only a sprain, so Nat walked on it for a year. Then another doctor re-broke the ankle and set it again. She wore a brace on her leg until the 1940s. From that time on, she had a limp and wore a steel plate in every shoe. She did not consider this a disability, never asked for any sympathy about her permanently altered gait, and certainly didn't let it slow her progress.

After completing advanced degrees, Nat took a position and taught at Missouri University (now University of Missouri-Columbia) from 1925-1935. While teaching there, Nat was continually networking to find staff for Camp Carry-On. She had worked very hard to develop the program and structure and was well on her way to becoming a year round, all-around educator of young women.

George Edwards was coach while she was at University of Missouri-Columbia. There were several basketball and football players taking her theory classes who were later renowned. Possibly advocating the extra-curricular programs she had been exposed to in NYC, here she started a tumbling club at night. First they had girls and then boys and, eventually, for the first time the students experienced co-educational P.E.

While Nat was at the UM-C, she was on the female coaching staff. Not one to worry about posing for formal photographs, she is 'not pictured'

A beautiful young lady, Natalie Wilson goes to the big city for more training

with six colleagues, in the yearbook. Her influence is noted in the copy on that page: "Interest in Golf has been stimulated by Miss Natalie Wilson…. She has supervision of Practice Teaching and coaches both indoor and outdoor baseball."

Here are some notes from Nat's discussion of early girls' basketball rules:

> The court was divided into three sections.
> "Centers" could only play in the middle.
> "Guards" were stationed to protect their own baskets.
> "Forwards" played in the section nearest the opposing team's basket.
> "Dribbling" was bouncing the ball once while moving.
> Being able to ricochet the ball off the backboard was a desirable skill.

At first, girls and boys had different sets of rules, but the games became more and more similar. By the time Nat was at the school at St. Louis' University City, the boys' rules had become the norm.

Tournament play was the only time teams traveled to compete. Most of the playing was done between the students at their home school "intramural." Girls especially only played with the locals. In colleges, different sororities would play against each other, etc. When they did take girls on the road there were chaperones along, but the girls would stay in homes where they played and "sometimes things got a little 'wild'". From Young Interview

Wall scaling was included in coursework while Nat taught at MU. Her tenure at MU lasted from 1925 to 1935, with two years as department head. Dr. Mary McKee,

Beautiful smiles on experienced college professors, and lifelong friends, Mary McKee and Nat Prussing

for whom the McKee Gymnasium on the MU campus was named, also served as chair of the P.E. department at the University of Missouri while Nat was teaching there. They remained lifelong friends.

Wall Climbing helps Captain Nat Put out the Fire —1925

The Tetley family lived in a clearing above Camp Carry-On situated on the Niangua River near Old Linn Creek. On a windy day, the roof of their house caught fire. Capt. Nat was sent for. In an interview in the 1990s, the Tetley's daughter recalled the experience when she was a young girl. "Captain Nat came, scaled the side of the house, and put out the fire." Big Nat, as the

Nat was a big fan of wall scaling. Hopefully, these photos will help the reader visualize her description of the process of getting a team of 12 girls up and over a twelve foot wall with no ladder!

reader will recall, had participated in climbing since her youngest days, including it in her camps and at UMC.

Acrobatic preparation for scaling the wall

Chapter Twelve

DEVELOPING CCO II

1927 was a banner year for Camp Carry-On in the press. In ten years Nat's successful camping program had grown popular, people took notice, and the number of campers continued to increase. Nat would look for a larger space very soon, but memories of the original Carry-On near Ha Ha Tonka were fresh in the minds of the campers and those who had taken part.

FORMER CAMP CARRY-ON GIRLS TO HOLD REUNION, *Columbia Missourian* March 3, 1927

A reunion banquet for all persons who have attended Camp Carry-On, a girl's camp located at Linn Creek in the Ozarks, will be held at the Coronado Hotel in St. Louis Saturday. Miss Natalie Wilson, instructor in the department of physical education of the University, is owner and director of the camp which was the first summer camp for girls established in the Central West.

The following from Columbia will attend the reunion: Miss Natalie Wilson and her mother from Warrensburg; Misses Carolyn Dziatzko, Jane Hunter and Nadia Fulks of the University; Susan Steuber of Stephens College; Helen Hickman of Christian College; Martha Smith, Mabel Cotton, Margaret Eleanor Proctor, Mary Martha Catron, Sally Barton, and Mary Conley; Miss Geneva Youngs, instructor of voice at the University who was at one time music counsellor at Camp Carry-On will also attend the reception. According to Miss Wilson, about 55 persons are expected to attend the banquet.

A poem composed for the reunion in 1927 gives several clues about the progress of the camp in its formative years, while also mentioning

The Young Women who are alumni of Camp Carry-On were called together for a reunion at the time the second camp was built. Nat's leadership style created loyal campers

every camper that had ever attended since the earliest days. Slightly edited as the nicknames lend few clues, it begins:

An Ode to Carry-On

"A way back in the days by gone
was founded a camp called Carry-On
And those little campers one and all,
their names today we must recall
And as their names I read to you,
may they pass before you in memories review.
In your memory fancy they may be khaki clad, Scratched and bare-
    kneed
They may be fat as butter or slender as a weed
They may be groomed to visit that "Y" camp at Niangwer
Or they may be dressed the hills to wander
They may be in overalls and a big straw hat.
They may be dressed for swimming or for bacon bat.
But be they playing in the river

104

Or in Nat's old Flivver,
we pause here and recall each one,
so none will be forgotten

So here's to Captain and her first crew
Their deeds were great, but their numbers few
They worked, they played,
they marched with a song.
It's due to their loyalty, camp lasted so long.
They were Alice and Nell, Mary and Marie
All but one have embarked on the matrimonial sea

In 1920 for captain and crew,
three tents were plenty for their needs
But it took all outdoors to answer for their deeds.
Caroline Aber from our home town and nine others
Would have stayed all year if they had their 'druthers.

This brings us to 1921.
And really the fun had just begun
For many of the old campers hit the trail back,
At least 29 campers in tents hit the sack.
So we all felt when Carry-On closed that year.
Of our howling success we had no fear
There came to us the following summer,
many old campers, and new . . . quite a number.
All was merry from sunset to sunrise. . . .
But all the girls woke to a surprise.
When all of a sudden one August morn,
we heard the honking of 7 taxi horns.
Every little camper had traveling clothes to don.
With tears chasing down their cheeks, bid fare-well to Carry-On

The next year [1925] was one of great renown,
That's the year a great singer came down.
So with Geva and many old camper and new,
that was a galley year for captain and crew.
Every tent was so full in 1926,

there wasn't a spare corner for a camper to stick
WE really had more than we dared to expect,
so some were put in the camp house annex.
In some ways 1926 led all the rest;
for that was the year Captain Kidd hid his chest.
The old campers tried and true
there came to us 19 that were brand new.
Can you beat that for a real camp???,
I don't think you can.

[after this point, the rhyme scheme is lost, here's an
humble swing at bringing the poem home--lai]

Only too soon came a day of confusion,
Traveling togs out, was it all an illusion?
Packing of bags, long-lost dress shoes and hats.
for the last time that summer the sounding of taps
Lights out—no sleep—talk and autograph rhymes.
Fast, frantic remembering of all the good times.

A hurried breakfast, over the hills horns toot—
tears, laughter, goodbyes—taxis scoot.
Tents down and folded the old house locked.
But ready for the coming year, we're here counting the clock.
Now here we are—All of Carry-On as we are able
sitting together at this grand banquet table.

The following story of the origin of the Treasure Hunt mentioned above was printed in an article in the May 21, 1927 Special Saturday Section of the *Columbia Missourian* by Ruby J. Cline.

"We often hear of the great consequence of little things. It was apparently a little thing when a native living across the river from Camp Carry-On presented the girls with a goat one summer, but that act led to what is now one of the most interesting features participated in by the Carry-On Campers.

Thirty girls at the camp that year became very fond of the goat, and gloom pervaded the camp when he disappeared one day. A systematic search was organized and carried out, but no goat was found. It was some two weeks later that the animal was spied by one of the children, silhouetted on the hill top back of the camp, and the whole camp dashed up the hill in response to the cry of "The Goat!" But the goat became frightened at the hue and cry, took to his heels and was never seen again by the girls. All that summer, however, when things became dull someone would say, 'Let's hunt the Goat!' So much enjoyment evolved from this pastime that it gave the idea to Miss Wilson, director of Carry On, which resulted in the Treasure Hunt, now a feature of the camp each summer.

Activities were first aid, horseback riding, dramatics, music, and rifle. A program of group competition is carried out between

CCO II, campers' cabin interior

Captain Nat taking notes

CCO Dramatices

the occupants of different tents and a shield awarded to the group that excels in art, music, hiking, swimming and tent inspection. To foster dramatics, there is a stunt night each week and for music, a song night to which gathering each tent group brings an original song each week. Many people consider the singing done at CCO its most outstanding feature, and of course it is by no means confined to Song Night. Singing is an important part of Sunday School held on the river bank each week. The girls sing again around the council fire on Sunday night, and on their hikes and during many other activities. Carry On has been called "The Singing Camp" and the constant singing expresses the spirit of the campers. To go on the 25 mile float trips on the Niangua, campers must pass a special swimming test, although the boats are poled by natives who know the river, a ducking is not uncommon."

A few months later when the Spring semester concluded, Nat was off again to the Ozarks. Another article appeared in the *Columbia Missourian*, July 6, 1927

LOCAL GIRLS IN CAMP CARRY ON: Nine Children from Here Are Taking Outing in Ozarks

Linn Creek, Mo.—Camp Carry-On, a summer camp for girls which is directed by Miss Natalie Wilson of the physical education department of the University of Missouri, has been open six days....

The camp site is a bluff and adjacent hollow surrounding Flat Rock Spring. The camp house, located on a bluff overlooking the Niangua is made of native lumber which was cut and sawed on the site. The cookhouse and dining hall for the campers is a stone building located near the spring. The campers are housed in one pole army tents, each of which houses five or six campers and a counselor.... A program of group competition is carried out between the occupants of the different cabins and a shield is awarded to the group that excels in art, music, hiking, swimming, and cabin inspection.

One of the features of the camp is the treasure hunt. The treasure chest, of walnut, is placed in an iron container and is shut by a padlock and chain. The whole is hidden somewhere in camp previous to the opening of camp. The chest carries a replica of what Captain Kidd's chest contained—nuggets of 'gold and silver,' spices and herbs, etc. The chest is looked for only by pairs and in the chest are two handmade silver pendants on a silver chain which the finders may keep. The emblem on the pendants is the insignia of the Order of Pirates [comprising the chest, its key, an overhanging tree and an animal which might be mistaken for a deer, but is likely the goat and only finders of the chest may be members].

The food at camp is prepared by two expert cooks, often one meal of the three is eaten away from the camp.

Hiking is one of the most popular sports because of so many interesting spots to be explored in this part of the Ozarks. One or more overnight hikes is given a week, and other popular features are the float trips on the Niangua River.

The highest individual award given at camp is the Henry Brown cup, a permanent silver loving cup which is kept in camp and each year the name of the best all-round camper is engraved on it. Columbia is well represented at camp this year. Those attending are: Helen Sarah Conley, Flora Katherine Conley, Mary Winston Conley, Sarah Gertrude Conley, Dorothy Jane Legget, Mary Elizabeth McMullan, Sally Barth, Virginia Estes, and Martha Gilliam. Camp Carry-On lasts until August 15.

The Henry Brown Loving Cup mentioned in the article was named for Henrietta Brown, a friend of Nat's from Sargent who lived in Long Island, New York. She was a beloved counselor at CCO for more than one summer while she was an instructor in the P.E. department of the

Floating the Niangua in homemade, hand crafted boats

University of Wisconsin. She presented the cup to the camp, and each year the best all-around camper's name was engraved upon the cup.

A Big Move

As the popularity of the camp grew, Nat began to search for a new location and soon found land to purchase nearby so that she could build a new improved campground. Concerning the first move of Camp Carry-On, Nat commented, "we had to move up the creek [Niangua] near Miller County." Although Nat did not know about it, plans were being made to construct the dam that created "The Lake of the Ozarks." Some who don't worry about the history of such things may be surprised to know that the Linn Creek of today is one of the many towns that physically moved to survive development of lakes, railroads, and roads. So, the "Old Linn Creek" where the first camp was located was about to be covered by rising waters that would make the lake.

While at the old Camp Carry-On, the girls had bunked in tents on wooden platforms, but the new camp would be developed with permanent structures. The campground was developed with buildings on native cobblestone foundations. Also of this stone, retaining walls and steps made the hillside more stable for the campers. Screened log cabins, a bathhouse, a lodge, and a beautiful activities area on the bank of the Niangua would provide a lovely and modern setting. The camp house was constructed in a modified style of the earliest Europeans who came to Missouri, the French fur traders and settlers. Upright logs set in earthen trenches, rather than stones, comprised the stockade type walls.

To build the second camp, Captain Nat needed some help, and a certain fellow from Warrensburg had begun making waves around Camden County. Max Prussing, the young boy on the white pony who rode by the Wilson Farm with his father's mounts for sale at the barns in downtown Warrensburg, had arrived in the area. He had built a wonderful log home place where later, as it would turn out, Nat would spend several years in a different part of the Ozark woods.

NEW LOCATION FOR Modern Camp on the Niangua River—*Star Journal,* January 13, 1928

Misses Youngs and Wilson Select Site in Camden County.

A new location for the camping summer has been announced for Camp Carry-On, a summer camp for girls conducted by Miss

Natalie Wilson of the women's physical education department of the University, and Miss Geneva Youngs of the School of Fine Arts.

The new camp is nine miles from (Old) Linn Creek, in Camden County, on the Niangua River and is three miles from the original camp ground.

The property has been bought by Miss Wilson and Miss Youngs, a new campsite has been laid out and cabins built. The camp will be completed by the last of June or the first of July, according to the owners."

Once Captain Nat Wilson had secured the land to build her new modern camp on the Niangua River, she knew the man to go to, Max Prussing. Nat had patterned her first camp on World War I army camps with barracks that were tents over stationary wooden platforms. This had been a common practice for camping for many years. But when the camp relocated the first time, she wanted the new camp to have cabins and a lodge built out of native lumber. Modern permanent buildings would replace the old fashioned camp where she had been renting land from Col. R.G. Scott who had come from Iowa around 1890. Col. Scott owned a large parcel of land including what is now known as Ha Ha Tonka State Park and Bridal Cave. In 1928, Nat moved upriver, buying 100 or so acres and hiring Max to build not only the buildings, but rock walls and a spring house. The result was a beautiful camp, with running water and generated electricity, certainly a new concept in the still rustic Ozarks.

The interior of the Captains quarters, where Nat was quite comfortable

After WWI, Max moved from Warrensburg to Linn Creek, the original county seat, near the confluence of the Niangua, Little Niangua, and Osage rivers. He opened a survey office and was well known in the area as a self-taught civil engineer. Little did they know that a year later, Union Electric of St. Louis (now Ameren) would buy up the land and build the Lake of the Ozarks. Max was hired as the head surveyor for the Lake Project. Nat sold her Camden County camp to Union Electric and hired Max to build the exact same camp on the Jack's Fork River near Mountain View. It was during this time (1933-34) that a budding romance started between Nat and Max. In August of 1935, they were married at Christ Episcopal Cathedral in St. Louis.

Camp Carry-On's program was fairly consistent throughout its years of activity. One only needs to examine the Sargent School Camp Bulletin to see the impact of the philosophy of that educator on her camping goals: According to Sargent himself in the 1912 booklet:

> Some 20 or 30 years ago, in connection with my college work, I made a series of physical examinations of professional athletes. Nearly every one of these men, who had become especially distinguished, attributed his ability largely to his mother's fine physique. History is replete with the names of famous men in every walk of life who attribute their success in a great measure to the character and ability of their mother. And now the latest researches of science into the laws of heredity assign to woman the most important function in procreation. Truly as Emerson says, 'Men are what their mothers made them.' Although women constitute one-half of the human race and are largely responsible for its upbuilding, they have a right to a health education for their own sakes as human beings. This does not mean that women are to be physically educated like men, or that they are to aspire to have large muscles and make athletic records. The highest ideals in physical development call for the manly man and the womanly woman, each being a complement to the other.

His words seem a bit dated today. By her example, though, there is no question that Captain Nat was devoted to improving the life and health of every girl (and boy) who came across her path or into her camp. Wherever Natalie was at the time she would recruit new leaders and workers. She also relied on her old friends from Warrensburg. Many of the Carry-On counselors were from University of Missouri-Columbia until the camp closed for the last time due to World War II in 1942.

The earliest promotional brochure for the camp was a single sheet of paper folded. As the camp became more successful and moved to larger quarters, a new style of "folder" was produced. The Camp Carry-On Booklet (ca. 1928) is a beautifully designed 10-page folder, with photos of the new camp. After the move, the line "Somewhere in the Ozarks" is added to the cover. The text describes directions to camp in terms somewhat unfamiliar today, since the passenger railways mentioned are no longer available. By 1928, though, several travel options were available to the girls, who were almost entirely by then from Webster Grove, or thereabouts, near St. Louis. "Carry-On is reached by automobile over United States Highway number 54. The Railway connections are the Rock Island at Versailles, Missouri or the Frisco [St Louis and San Francisco Railway] at Lebanon, Missouri. Campers are met at these stations and brought to camp by the Carry-On bus."

The facilities are described and the Aims stated. Parents and campers who might worry are comforted by the security of the remote new location:

> The Camp property of one hundred and fifty acres with its woods and streams and meadows assures privacy and makes an interesting place where Campers can enjoy roaming and riding

Clay Court tennis tournaments were held at CCO

in perfect safety. The camp buildings are ideally situated on the hillsides fronting the river, affording south, east, and west exposure. There is an athletic field equipped for tennis, volleyball and baseball. An outdoor theatre nestled among the cedars is one of the beauty spots of the camp. The swimming 'hole' is very accessible. It has a diving board and floats as well as ample room for the shallow water swimmers.

But time at this new camp was short. An article from the St. Louis Globe Democrat, January 21, 1926 was reprinted in the book *Before the Dam Water* by T. Victor Jefferies, an attorney and local proponent of the dam. The article conveys information about Linn Creek. The town was once a thriving port "furnishing supplies for hundreds of miles into the Southwest" on the confluence of the Osage and Niangua Rivers before it was submerged in the new lake:

"Night is falling over the Ozarks. The red sun has long since dropped behind the ridge and the western horizon is in a halo into which is etched the silhouette of scraggling pines and here and there a lonely farmhouse. A fascinating picture with all the lonesomeness that it conveys."

From here on the incredibly colorful and descriptive words of Louis LaCoss, the reporter, will be summarized for the modern reader.

A camp reunion at Mrs. Nat Prussing's new home, Tall Timbers

CCO II View, showing stacked rock walls

Louis and company had "commandeered" a taxi to take them the thirty miles from the last railroad station to Linn Creek. The driver talked constantly over the racket of the "ancient Ford, which he propelled over the road at imminent danger of life and limb." He anticipated their doom, over "mile upon mile of clattering over a muddy highway, a brief respite at the Bagnell Ferry" where their "taxi" coughed and sputtered until they reached the other side of the river with a view of the twinkling lights of the town in the valley under starry skies and velvety black mountains.

"'There she is—little old Linn Creek, at your service.' In his enthusiasm, the driver took his hands from the wheel, nearly pitching the whole car over a cliff into Linn Creek, in the opinion of the passenger. But soon enough they were on Main Street, with the taxi gasping its last in front of the Hotel."

The purpose of their trip was to interview some of the 500 residents of the "doomed" village that would vanish without a trace. The Missouri Hydroelectric Power Company, a Kansas City concern in a power project that would affect the counties of Camden, Miller, Morgan, and Benton, proposed creating a huge dam that would cross and stop the Osage River three miles above the town of Bagnell. The resulting lake would have 1,000 miles of shoreline. $1,800,000 had already been spent and the Missouri Public Service Commission had been asked permission to sell 19 million dollars more in bonds to pay for the project.

The entire country surrounding Linn Creek was a paradise of forests and flowers and breathtaking scenery. Rugged peaks, deep canyons,

CCO II, The dining hall was a place for food and friendship

and rushing streams were found there. So primitive was the region that there are only a few tiny villages within and rails, the closest twenty miles away at Bagnell. A thirty mile drive took over an hour.

In the 1820s, explorers pushed up the Osage River and a town, first called Kinderhook, was built at the intersection of the rivers, a county seat with no rivals for the honor. Linn Creek's heyday was just before the Civil War in the 1850s when it was the upper terminus of the Osage River's huge traffic flow. Goods shipped to Linn Creek from Liverpool, England, never touched land until they were safely in the warehouses there. The goods were transferred from ocean liners at New Orleans and up the Mississippi River to St. Louis and then up the Missouri River to the Osage. Great fleets of small craft were in service with gigantic amounts of river traffic until the railroads came and it all ended.

As the reporter was sitting down to a dinner, even he, almost 100 years ago, felt a longing for the past that was filled by the quaint village that was Old Linn Creek:

> For the benefit of those who perchance have grown tired of 'restaurant cooking' and the tasteless unpalatable concoctions that city chefs offer their patrons, it might not be amiss to re-call: the aroma of sizzling ham, huge platters of it for the taking.

CCO II Float!

Roast ribs of pork swimming in their gravy. Mashed potatoes and fried; dried corn and fried cabbage; macaroni and cheese; baked beans; hash whose authenticity could not be doubted; pickles and relishes, homemade apple, peach, plum and pear preserves; tumblers of sweet milk and mugs of steaming coffee, and three kinds of pie. Heaping dishes were there to be dipped into at will.

At the time of the article, people of the town were still uncertain as to whether the dam would be built, regardless of all the money spent by the power companies, and the plans being made in the power centers of the state. The very day La Coss was in Linn Creek there was a meeting and the sheriff spoke:

"Clayburn (of Decaterville) was plum agin it. He riz right up in meeting and he says, says he 'Gentlemen, my district is agin this thing and I'm not agoin' to vote for it.' Tom Edwards of Mack's Creek said his district favored it a bit, but Leonard Franklin, the presiding judge, said he wasn't agoin' to take any sides just yet. 'Gentlemen, it took more than twenty days for you fellers to get a decision in Jefferson City and I'll be dadburned if you're agoin' to come down here and get us to make a decision in half a day... No Siree!'"

One of several CCO II cabins that are used as lake houses to this day

CCO II cabin today

The issue was tabled until the first of February. Sentiment in the community was half and half, and no one was sure what would happen. It's no wonder that Nat had gone on with building the camp in 1928.

A copy of a letter Nat wrote in February of 1931 survives concerning an issue in Camden County that resulted in an unexpectedly quick trip to meet the Commissioners. "We truly appreciate your kind offer and may call on you again later on. The case as it stands now gives us no idea as to when it is apt to be tried in court, but we do expect it to happen before the middle of March or the first of April. Thanking you again for your interest in our case."

In the book Before the Dam Water, an article from March 5, 1931 laments:

CCO II Springhouse today

Town Near Doom… The little town is in ruins. In a week or two all that remains of it will be at the bottom of a lake, fifty feet deep. The courthouse, the bank, the First Baptist Church and the old homes where babies were born and elders died are little squares and rectangles of broken brick and stone. They are just like ruins dug up from lava beds and deserts. Only the steps remain. One may sit upon them and brood on the desolate valley before the water comes.

In 2008, Nat Jr. contacted the present owners of the second Camp Carry-On "Camp House" on the Niangua River. It has been lakefront living quarters for Terall and Shirley Siddons since the 1970s. Much of the structure of the camp remains, including shower house, spring house, several modified cabins, and the beautiful stonework that is nearly 100 years in place.

Captain Nat learned that when Bagnell Dam created the Niangua Arm of the Lake of the Ozarks, it would put most of the new Prussing-built Camp Carry-On under water. She never knew that it had become lakefront property. All the buildings and the spring house have stood the test of time and are in 2017 almost all inhabited by lake dwellers. The "mess hall" is the finest of these and has been restored and remodeled a bit. One of the loveliest features of the camp in modern times are native stone walls. The current owners, said when they purchased the land, the walls were covered with vines and completely obscured. The girl's quarters are now lakeside cabins.

Chapter Thirteen

European Trip for Miss Wilson

"The Great Depression" deepened in the early 1930s, and there were many bank failures. By 1933 depositors saw most of their money lost, and most banks had closed their doors. Nat had planned and booked reservations for a summer physical education tour of Europe. She was one of a group of women educators interested in advanced training skills being used there, especially in Germany. Because of the bank closings, only two women had withdrawn their deposits out of the banks the year before, Nat being one. In 1933, Nat's horizons continued to expand when she took a Summer Education Tour in Europe. "When I took the European trip, we ended up having almost a private tour. All the others cancelled due to the banks failing, but I had already purchased my ticket before that happened."

The Burning of the Books
by Natalie Jr. Halpin

While in Berlin, two women went to the Berlin Opera on May 10th, 1933. Upon exiting, they left by the side door onto the Plaza, where

Centurion Cameo Nat purchased while visiting Italy. The setting with her initials was created by a jeweler upon her return to the States. In 1982, she gave Natalie Jr. the ring as a Christmas gift.

The burning of books by Hitler's troops on the Biblioplatz

70,000 people had gathered to see the famous "Burning of the Books." They saw Joseph Goebbels on a high platform speaking. His voice blasted out to the crowd while students and Hitler's troops and students were throwing over 20,000 volumes of "un-German" books into the fire in an act of ominous significance, thereby signifying an era of uncompromising state censorship. Goebbels was Hitler's minister of "Propaganda and Public Enlightenment."

Hitler's troops and students in the thirty-four state sponsored university towns across Germany burned books from German Jewish authors, such as Albert Einstein and Sigmund Freud, and of course American authors like Ernest Hemingway, Helen Keller, Sinclair Lewis, and more. Since 1995 on that site, called Bebelplatz, is a monument of sunken glass plate with a view underneath of a roomful of empty bookshelves. This artwork is by Israeli artist Micha Ullman and is called "Library." A plaque beside it quotes a Jewish poet, Heinrich Heine, who wrote 100 years before the book burnings: "Wherever books are burned, human beings are destined to be burned too."

Nat remembered going to see German athletes competing in the Berlin Sportpalast, a multipurpose indoor arena, which held 14,000. Later it was most famous for Joseph Goebbels's 1943 "Total War" Speech.

The peaceful countryside must have been a pleasant contrast

In Berlin, she also saw the arena, which would become the Olympic Stadium, but no one was there. A blond man said everyone had gone to the war games down at the women's building. [Natalie Jr. believes those arenas were part of Hitler's rise in power and that the stadium used for the 1936 Olympics was being built in 1933. The International Olympic Committee in April of 1931 voted to hold the Olympics in Berlin.]

Captain Nat said, "We stayed in a house in the suburbs of Berlin with a Jewish family. They were wonderful hosts. The mother had been educated in France, and the son spoke English. Their older daughter was a teacher, but Jewish people had already started to lose their jobs in Germany...." One day when they came back to their street, there were big vans in the way and soldiers blocking the ends of the street. The soldiers had been into homes and were taking silver. Dissidents had begun to be rounded up. She often wondered what had happened to them during the war. Were they able to escape? Were they taken to a Nazi concentration camp? Did they survive? Six million Jewish people were killed by Hitler's regime in World War II.

In Copenhagen, Denmark, a choreographed demonstration of Hoop Rolling was a highlight, as was "a lariat demonstration where 50 girls threw ropes in perfect unison for a routine."—this and following information came from the taped Young interview.

Nat noted several other interesting educational techniques and state-of-the-art facilities that they saw. "In Sweden, the balance beam was popular. We had those at Sargent and at the Normal, but they had been low and in this country the beams were high in the air."

Finnish baseball was interesting because they had no pitcher. The batter just threw their own pitch straight up in the air and hit it on the way down. One of her souvenirs was a Finnish bat.

Nat said she stood only twenty feet from a public bonfire of books, where Hitler was present. After witnessing this, she and her fellow traveler only knew the number of the bus that they had arrived on and had a difficult time finding their way back to it. It was by remembering the colors of the tablecloths at the little outdoor cafes that the women found their way back. The red and white checkered ones caught their eye. Then, finally, they found the #5 bus.

Chapter Fourteen

BECOMING JUDGE MAX PRUSSING OF TALL TIMBERS

After Max completed his service with the American Expeditionary Forces, he returned to and graduated from UCM (still "Normal #2"). Part of the time he lived in Johnson County's Old Courthouse, which had been converted into a boarding house.

At approximately the same time, Max was improving and building the farm complex that his daughter, Natalie Halpin, donated to the university in 2002 as the Prussing Research Farm of the Agriculture department. He built the family

Interior of the Prussing Barn, built in 1902

home with a slate roof in 1921 (still watertight after a century). Before he was finished improving his father's farm, Max had also added a scale barn, workshop, and a bi-level barn for implements and cattle. Other building projects were a smoke house, wood shed, and chicken house. These structures are still standing as of 2017.

Farming with his father did not prove satisfactory, so Max embarked on another route which would take advantage of his education. After leaving for the Ozarks in 1923, Max first opened a survey office in Linn Creek with Ralph Vincent. He became a civil engineer and was appointed in 1929 as chief surveyor for the Lake of the Ozarks project by Union Electric of St. Louis, working with Wes

Interior of the hayloft of the Prussing Barn today.

McAfee, then the President of U.E. As Bagnell Dam created the lake, the rising waters would flood the original county seat where his office had been located.

Beginning July 29, 1929, the lovely little county seat of Linn Creek, population about 400, changed forever as witnessed by both Max and Nat. Union Electric received authorization from the Missouri Public Service Commission to begin the construction of Bagnell Dam—"the world's largest, privately-owned hydro-electric plant." At least it was then. The estimated cost was 30 million dollars. The plans had first been considered in 1912, but research and planning took a long time. Nine days after approval, the work began, employing 180 men. Twenty thousand would be needed to complete the project. As the only such project to begin at the advent of the Great Depression, lines were long for the jobs. Men came from the East where the stock market crash hit first and hardest.

Long term benefits proposed by the builders weren't making the locals very happy. Construction began on bunkhouses, cottages, and a mess hall. One representative number of the impact on the sparsely populated Ozark hills: the Union Electric Mess served 600,000 meals before the project was completed. Bagnell Dam supplied urgently needed power to homes and businesses in St. Louis and other communities in Iowa, Missouri, and Illinois. For many years, it was the primary power source in St. Louis.

Max Prussing, his survey office having been located in Old Linn Creek, was involved in the Bagnell Dam/Lake of the Ozarks project as a civil engineer from start to finish.

Former residents of Linn Creek had to move. Some started New Linn Creek; others moved a bit further away to build a new and better town "Camdenton."

Max engraved his initials on a feed bin he built for the barn

Panoramic view of the Prussing Farm today

Preparation for construction began August 6th, 1929. The first concrete on Bagnell Dam was poured in April of 1930. In less than ten months, the lake began to fill reaching spillway elevation on May 20, 1931. That year Highway 54 traffic began to cross the bridge.

At first the banks wouldn't loan money on the property that would later be the "lakefront." Locals said it would be swampy and festering with mosquitos and unhealthy air. But the air cleared as the lake filled, and by 1980, the cost of a square foot of lakefront property was $300 or 13 million dollars an acre. Thirty-five years later, in 2015, cost per square foot had at least tripled in value.

Interior of the scale house today, this building was used to weigh wagon loads of grain and livestock, too.

Max was then hired to design and build the new county seat—Camdenton. With urban planning of his chosen design, the modern town was built in concentric circles with the courthouse in the center and the business district in the first ring around that. "All fireproof, not to cost less than $2000." The next circle was to contain homes, "none costing less than $1,500." Later he would be elected and serve as presiding judge (now known as commissioner) of Camden County until 1941.

When Hurricane Deck Bridge was completed and dedicated in October 1937, photos appeared in the Kansas City Times. The Bridge won

Up to date design of the courthouse by Victor J. DeFoe, architect, overseen by Judge Max and completed in 1931

The dam under construction… note the railroad tracks used in the process

an award at the time of its construction as "The Most Beautiful Bridge" built that year in the United States:

A metal plaque awarded by the American Institute of Steel Construction, which sponsors the annual design awards, was received at the ceremonies by Judge M.M. Prussing of Camdenton, presiding judge of the Camden County court, who assisted by Governor Stark, bolted the award to the bridge structure… Excepting the Golden Gate Bridge in California, no other structure in the country has a deeper pier than Number 5 of the Hurricane Deck bridge. That pier stands in eighty-seven feet of water in the Lake of the Ozarks.

An article in 1999 admitted that though the bridge improved the quality of life for residents and visitors, the tolls collected to cross it

Views from above the dam construction

Bridge dedication and award for Design at the Lake of the Ozarks, Hurricane Deck Bridge, Governor Lloyd Crow Stark and Judge Max

had not ever been enough to pay for the original construction. The toll was lifted, and the bridge turned over to the Missouri Highway Department in 1953.

Even while he was busy in Camden County, Max was still training and riding fine saddle horses back on the home place in Warrensburg. Max purchased a horse called Dan Patch from his friend Ben Grover. He later sold the horse to a well-known Warrensburg horse man, Walter Jones, who sent many mules overseas for the war from his railyard-adjacent Jones Mule Barn. Jones knew horses, and he wanted Dan Patch for his daughter Marion. In 1933 and 1934, a World's Fair called "A Century of Progress" was held on the occasion of the Centennial of Chicago. Max trained such a fine mount that Miss Marion Jones' Dan Patch won several blue ribbons.

"You're not going to vote in MY County!!!"
by Natalie Jr. Halpin

In 1934 Max Prussing turned away two busloads of non-residents who hoped their votes would influence a state-wide election by voting in Camden County. These fraudulent voters had traveled from a distance and Max Prussing was the elected Presiding Judge in Camden County.

In the 1930s, Tom Pendergast was the political boss of Kansas City and Jackson County and had power in much of the state. He controlled the voting in many areas, sending busloads of illegal voters into the Ozarks. When Max got word of two busses traveling down Highway 5 from Versailles, he was ready for them, blocking the road with his black Dodge pickup truck. When the buses were forced to stop, Max motioned the lead driver to come over. The driver was yelling for Max to get out of the road and came to Max's open truck door. Max told him to turn around the buses and go back to Kansas City—they were not going to vote in his county. When the driver said otherwise, Max stepped out of

Nat Jr. brings shining smiles and contagious laughs to Tall Timbers

the truck with his Colt revolver in his right hand and slammed it over the man's head. The buses turned around and were gone in a flash! Political boss Tom Pendergast never fooled with Camden County again.

Max had really settled in to Camden County since building his beloved home in the woods. Max's secluded homestead and farm, Tall Timbers, had expanded and featured several specially designed outbuildings on seventy acres. There was a main house, a guest house, a double car garage with an apartment, a large barn, an electric generator house, and a well house.

As if he didn't have enough on his plate, Max served on the Board of Regents for UCM, at that time called Central Missouri State Teachers College.

There was now a new location for the Camp Carry-On reunions at Tall Timbers.

When he and Nat were married Tall Timbers became their convivial home. Little Nat came into the picture soon after and so the family grew, staying in the woods of Camden County from 1938-1942, when Big Nat, Little Nat, and cousin John Wilson would move back to Hurricane Hill.

From 1938 until 1942, Max served on the University of Central Missouri's Board of Regents in Warrensburg.

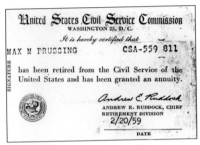

After Max's retirement he receive an annuity for his service to the United States

Still keeping up his certification in 1963.

Max and Friend Ben Grover, with Dan Patch, the horse on the right. The building behind them is the scale barn

Chapter Fifteen

CARRY-ON SOUTHWARD

CCO III—Mountain View

Camp Carry-On continued to fill the "days off" from Captain Nat's career in education. Two months of the year, as long as it was possible, Nat went back into the woods and encouraged her girls to rise to whatever challenges they might face. She was a very good example, riding with the current, always on the lookout for the next change of course.

Eventually, Nat was informed that the ever-growing lake would submerge the new camp in Camden County, necessitating another move; Nat was not at all discouraged. Camp Carry-On was relocated over 120 miles away, a journey of three-and-a-half hours from Warrensburg on gravel, before the efficient roads of today, and she never looked back. Of course it would be Max who built another new camp very similar to

Lodge, Camp Carry-On on the Jack's Fork

the one they had just created at a new location on the Jack's Fork River near Mountain View, Missouri.

Reunions would continue, first at Tall Timbers and later on Hurricane Hill, as the girls kept in touch with lifelong friends made just as Nat had intended when she formed the very first camp. Her influence was also lifelong, as a number of poems, songs, and letters attest:

A poem:
Ah dear Captain Nat of Carry-On
We love you for your loyalty and kindness all along
We shall always find in you a true companion
For 'twas your patient fond endeavor made us strong.
So From now on we shall follow your example
Knowing surely you will show us what is best
We are sure we will never find a friend more faultless
And we know we feel just as the rest.

In 1934, when the camp moved to Mountain View, Nat wrote a letter to all the former campers telling them of the new home for Carry-On. Letters back from several of the girls lamented that they were too old to go to camp themselves, and many were working and longing for those lovely summers past. Everyone who wrote had thought of at least one girl who would be improved by attending Camp Carry-On. But each girl also mentioned—remember that the Depression was in full swing at about this time—that money was a concern in their home communities.

Julia Sikes, a Carry-On camper, was a lifelong friend of Nat. Two of her letters were kept, one from 1934 and the other almost fifty years later in 1983 for Nat's 90th birthday. The early letter credits Nat with fine leadership and announces a new arrival.

Dearest Nat, Do you know my latest? John and I have a baby girl! Oh it's grand—she is the sweetest, cutest thing you ever laid your eyes on, and—she'll be a camper some day. Don't you forget it! For all the little good in me I give thanks to YOU. You brought forth that which I thot couldn't be brought forth…. As to your new camp—I'm so pleased that you are startin' again and I'll do my level best to send you some body or several.

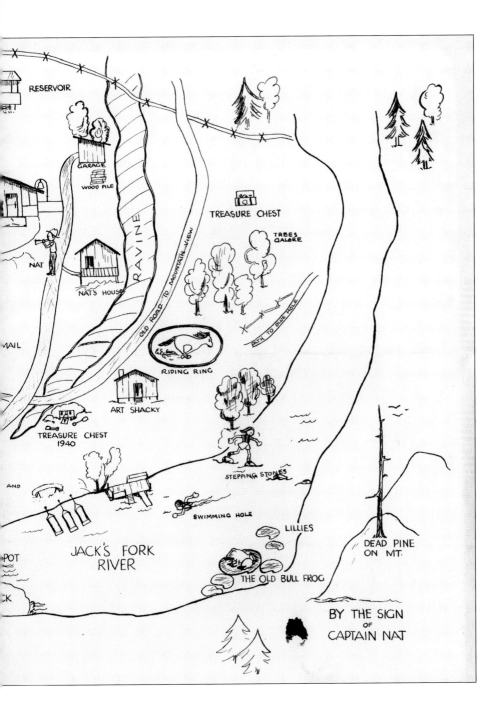

Please do send me some literature—and here are a few names: Mary Jane Sikes, Betty and Peggy Donnell, Eleanor Harty, Helen Vera Dudley, Inez Hollingsworth, Rosemary Blanton, Esther Jane Greer.

You know you are getting closer to our country. Mountain View is west of here. I hope we can come visit you and look it over. Here's hoping you have a grand year and my best love to you. —Julia K. Sikes, Feb 15, 1934

Later, she had been married for fifty years by this time, Julia wrote:

Dear Nat: How nice after all these years, to say hello to you on your birthday. What wonderful memories I have of my four years at Camp Carry-On and what a splendid leader you were (at times I didn't think so)… John and I send our love.

Enclosed in the letter were a photo of Julia and John in 1926 and a clipping from their 50th in 1979. In the photo John wears a full swimsuit with a Red Cross symbol and Julia is dressed in hiking togs. Julia Sikes was born July 4th, 1909 in Boonville, Cooper County, Missouri; she died June 1, 1988 in Sikeston, Scott County, Missouri.

Uniforms are similar to the earlier camps, but more knees showing

Letter from a Satisfied Mother –Lexington, Missouri, July 31, 1935.

Dear Miss Wilson: We thoroughly enjoyed our visit with you at Camp Carry On. It is a beautiful place, so quiet and restful and since our return I have found myself many times wishing I were there again enjoying your lovely shade and cool breezes.

We were greatly perplexed when we went down over Bitsy, and thinking we should have discussed with you more fully just what we should do about her staying on. I hope you thought we were right in our decision. I am sure she is more than happy. Her letters have been so brightly like herself. The climax coming with the finding of the chest! I hope you can tell how very deeply we appreciate this wonderful opportunity you have given her. It will always be a 'challenge' and inspiration to her all through life to have come in contact and known you and your efficient and lovely counselors. My sincerest regards to each one of them and many thanks to all.

Most sincerely yours, Nancy Lee Dell

The *Star Journal*, June 13, 1935 reported that Natalie Wilson left for Camp Carry-On at Mountain View with Lem Shattuck her little nephew, opening July 1.

Miss Natalie Wilson weds Max Prussing
Star Journal August 18, 1935

Miss Natalie Wilson, youngest daughter of Mr. and Mrs. J.H. Wilson, and Judge Max Prussing of Camdenton were married early Sunday morning in Christ Church Cathedral in St. Louis. They are spending a few days in St. Louis before returning to the country home of Judge Prussing, six miles west of Camdenton.

The wedding came as a surprise to their friends at this time although it was known they were to be married soon. Because Judge Prussing is not able to be away from his work, they are planning a western trip later in the fall. Mrs. Prussing has been at her home here for the past week after the close of her girl's camp near Mountain View. She recently resigned her position as assistant professor in the department of physical education at the University of Missouri, which she has held for several years. She formerly taught in the public schools of San Antonio and in the College here.

Sue Hubbell, *New York Times*-bestselling author of *The Secret Life of Bees*, described the location of the campground in a *New York Times* article, reprinted in the *Kansas City Star*, Sun-

Target practice was part of the program, and no one thought a thing was wrong. Lem at right.

day April 13, 2003. Hubbell had started keeping bees near Mountain View in the 1970s. Since then, it has become a Missouri conservation area, and she is happy that it is accessible to all. She had visited the place in the early 2000s after being gone several years and wrote of its natural beauty:

> A young chipmunk, who had never seen a human, sat down a foot from me and tried to figure me out. When I shifted position, it wisely scuttled. The cheerful, lobed green leaves growing perpendicular to the cliff walls promised columbine blossoms in early summer. A favorite stand of equisetum, a primitive plant, was still there, reminding me that some species can last for eons.
>
> I climbed down to the Blue Hole, just above the old girl's camp and arguably the prettiest spot on the Jacks Fork River. It is at a turn, a wide deep pool, its depth so great that swimmers attempting to measure it come up gasping, the bottom never reached. Local people call it the "Gar Hole" because those big toothy fish live in it. I sat on the gravel bar beside it, looked in vain for green and great blue herons. Probably too early for them. [The area is on the Mississippi flyway for migrating birds and that day she recalled seeing almost 200 species in her time on the farm.]
>
> The woods around the Blue Hole and the girls' camp below were carpeted with wildflowers. I walked back up the eroded trail that at the turn of the 20th century had served as the road to the camp.

In April of 1937, the patriarch of the Hurricane Hill family died suddenly. As reported in his obituary:

J. H. Wilson, Dies Suddenly—Former Mayor Found Dead by Wife on Floor in Bath Room—Former Businessman was appointed County Collector by Gov. Hyde.

Friends of Wilson were shocked Thursday Morning to learn of his sudden death at his home, Hurricane Hill. Although his health had not been good for several months, Mr. Wilson had not been confined to his bed and spent Wednesday working on the lawn. When he did not appear for breakfast Mrs. Wilson went to investigate and found him dead on the floor. Death had occurred a short time before, probably from a stroke.

The family gathered, except for Mary O's family who was on the way to Europe onboard an ocean liner and son, John, who was living in California and not expected to return.

"The July 2, 1937 *Daily Star Journal* reported that Louise Martin, P.E. Instructor at UCM and, Nat's Mother, Mrs. J.H. Wilson left to contribute their talents to Camp Carry-On." It takes many dedicated leaders to manage the activities of young campers. Elma's help is no surprise, as she clearly was an avid supporter of her children's efforts. And always on the lookout for new counselors and teachers, Louise Martin was a great choice. In 1923 Nat filled a position at UCM just before the arrival of Louise Martin, who remained Head of the Women's P.E. Department at the College until June 30, 1954.

In 1938 it was back to the Jack's Fork for Captain Nat, and this time, there was a sweet addition to the camp. Nat informed the campers by letter that she and Max had a beautiful little girl, Natalie Jr.

Nat received a letter before camp from Lem Jr. "Dear Nat, I have decided that I want to come down to Carry-On. That is, if you want me. In the first place, it's nearly time. In the second place I want to see the old campers and Nat Jr. How are you and Unkle Max and the baby? Please tell Unkle Max to have another lawn mower sent out. Your Nephew, Lem Jr. P.S. Please answer."

A map of the camp from the later years [see p.136] shows how beloved their baby girl was. "Nat Jr.s Sandpile" has taken a place in the camp layout. It is certain that the little blonde-haired, blue-eyed doll was well loved by Captain Nat's devoted campers. As they grew, she and her cousin Lem Shattuck took full advantage of the activities of the camp. Somehow, it seems a sentimental and fitting repetition of Natalie Sr. and John's adventures as they enjoyed Ha Ha Tonka in the not-so-distant past.

Natalie Wilson Prussing, "Little Nat" was born January 5th, 1938 and would be the delight of her parents throughout their lives and a great help in their later years. Inspired no-nonsense mothering was right in Nat's wheelhouse. Choosing not to

Nat Jr. on her horse, Dynamite

choose between motherhood and a career, she immediately designed the new camp with her daughter in mind. One imagines that among a group of energetic young ladies, there was no shortage of volunteer babysitters. An alternate childcare plan was available to this busy mother in a gentle giant of a horse named Dynamite! She would plop Little Nat astride that horse, happy as can be, for hours at a time. One of the loveliest pictures at this time is Natalie Jr. in the washtub, barefoot, wearing overalls. Her little smiling face shows exquisite happi-

1938 Tall Timbers, CCO reunion. Nat, in the hat, holding Nat Jr. on her lap

ness in the primitive conditions. It must have been that optimism she inherited from her dynamic parents.

Dr. Nat and the Moonshiner
by Natalie Jr. Halpin

In the 1930s there were many bootleggers in the Missouri Ozarks. One such moonshiner lived up the Ridge from Camp Carry-On. On a hot afternoon the man's wife came running into camp. "Where is Dr. Nat? Where is Dr. Nat?" Upon hearing the cry, Nat immediately picked up her medicine bag and heeded the call to follow the woman into the brush above the Jack's Fork River. She found the bootlegger lying on a cot near his still, with a wide gash from the front to the back of the man's skull. From a cliff he had dived into the Jack's Fork and cut his

Captain and Nat Jr. at CCO III

head wide open on a big rock. The blood was gushing. Nat knew the Hill Folk thought she was a doctor and could fix anything. She reported later that there was only one way to close the wound. Disinfect the area and braid his hair together, which was long and greasy. It worked, and he was back to producing his "white lightnin'" in no time at all, very grateful to Dr. Nat.

Excerpts Camp Newspaper from Camp Carry-On at Mountain View
The Gadabout, July 1940
Editorial

Did you ever stop to think that you are taking a great deal of nature for granted? One can find beauty in everything and it all depends on how much you yourself wish to get out of this life of yours.

Do you remember the glory of the sunset on our last overnight hike? I wonder if you stopped to think of the many colors changing in that scene? With the dusk came the night bringing a cool fragrance to all of us. The trees silhouetted against the sky were an unforgettable sight.

For me this beauty contained a double meaning because it was my last overnight hike as a 1940 Carry-On Camper. I am very grateful for the fun and friendship I have had among all of you CCO's. Camp Carry-On will always be the one and only camp for me. Your editor, Mary Hardy

Society notes:

All of us campers were on hand to greet Max when he drove into camp last Saturday noon. We were mighty glad to see him, especially Nat Jr. who ran from the art shack to meet him.

A birthday is a gala occasion at camp. At least Tiny's proved to be. She received everything from a kiss delivered by Bunny to some presents given by the campers and counselors. Tuesday night the dining room became a place of festivity as Nat led Tiny to a surprise dinner. AND, we had a beautiful white cake with pink candles. Or maybe I should say Tiny had the cake. All in all, a good time was had by everyone. Here's to bigger and better birthdays to come.

Well, our overnight hike up the mountain last Monday night brought on an awful lot of chiggers and a few ticks, but it was really worth all the discomfort of itching bites. In spite of the awful climbing and dangling over cliffs, stories that we heard declared the trip a thrilling experience. (All goes to show you just can't believe everything you hear.)

Were we surprised when a cute little collie dog wandered into camp last Tuesday? We gave him a bath to take the ticks and bugs off, and he now resides in Cabin six. P.S. We haven't decided on a name for him yet.

Oh, yes, Jim and Vivian were down Wednesday night to sing for us.

That's about all for this week. See you at Caravan,

Your Society Editor.

The Gadabout came out at regular intervals during camp. It was typewritten, probably on an old system that used lightweight paper stencils, and then it would be reproduced in multiples on a machine, almost incomprehensible today, called a "duplicating machine". No auto-correct—if you typed a mistake into the stencil, you had to either start over or be satisfied with reproducing your mistakes. The articles have been edited for spelling and other "typos"—a.k.a. typographical errors.

After the summer of 1941, Carry-On would be no more. In December of 1941, the United States entered World War II. The intrepid Captain Nat had every intention to reopen in 1946, but by then, the tornado had wiped it out. On

When the tornado came through the camp, only three canoes, and the English China service had survived. These are still used by Natalie Jr. when she entertains in her parents' home.

inspection by Max, all that was left were the toilets standing bare on a hill, three canoes, and the English chinaware. Much of the china is still used by Natalie Jr.

Going to Mountain View in the Camp Truck

Nat on the tractor

Max with Colonel

Act III
FOLLOWING THEIR HEARTS

Chapter Sixteen

THE OZARKS CATCH FIRE

Nat was still living at Tall Timbers with Max and Natalie Jr. while conducting camp Carry-On each summer on the Jack's Fork. Their lives were filled with wonder, continuing the exploration and love of nature that had been a signature of Captain Nat's life. Max's work had evolved as he oversaw the building of Fort Leonard Wood.

Lem Shattuck, Nat Jr. and John Wilson at Tall Timbers, ca. 1942

"Old timers will long remember Easter Sunday 1941 as "Black Sunday" in the Ozarks. The right combination came together that day—prolonged drought, high temperatures, low humidity, 55 mph winds and a few kitchen matches. For 24 hours it seemed as if the whole Ozarks was on fire."

–*Missouri Conservationist* magazine, September 2000.

Out of the Woods
by Natalie Jr. Halpin
Published in "The Long Journey" ©2001 Dr. Robert Jones' Warrensburg Writers Circle

"Get in the car! Get in the car!" my mother yelled to my cousin and me. It was the middle of the night when she aroused us from a deep sleep with this shout, sending fear through us.

I was three and a half and my cousin was six years old and we knew my mother meant NOW! We jumped into the old Dodge car as my mother said, "I'm going for help, the wind has come up, and the charging forest fire is headed in our direction."

We lived in the Ozarks, five miles from Camdenton. Grandmother Elma had appropriately named our seventy acres "Tall Timbers". The trees towered dense around us and all the buildings were made of hand hewn logs with wood shingled roofs, much like the buildings of Camp Carry-On, also built by my father. Our homestead contained a barn, pump house with electrical generator, a well house, a two car garage, a guest house and the main house. A person could actually walk into the cavernous fireplace. That fireplace heated the whole house, so a woodpile with the winter's supply of firewood was stacked 30 feet from the front door.

Our driveway leading to graveled Highway 5 was a quarter mile in length and as we approached the gate at a high rate of speed, we could see that the wooden cattle guard was ablaze. Mother said, "Hang on, we're going over", and we did, like a streak of lightning. Fortunately, the cattle guard, made of green boards of 2x4 oak did not burn easily... and nothing in the car caught fire.

Mother drove to several neighbor's houses and a man in each house said he would be over to help fight the fire. So, back we went, over the flaming pit. By now the fire had spread and seemed to be everywhere.

The spring of 1941 had been the driest in decades and the Forest Rangers were fighting fires all over the Missouri Ozarks. The nearby fire tower was vacant and without a telephone, we could only hope for neighbors' help and a change of wind direction or rain to save Tall Timbers. But who could see the sky? There was only fire and smoke.

Mother deposited John and me at the house and said, "go inside and stay put!" She started fighting the fire with a hose, bucket, shovel and a rake. The neighbor men arrived and started bucketing water from the well to the fire. There was no progress in containing the raging flames.

I was scared to stay in the house and my cousin was curious, so outside we went. Oh, the smoke hit us like a blanket and I began to cry. All I remember is Mother shouting, "get back in that house, both of you!" We both just stood there, watching the fire getting closer and closer. Suddenly, I felt something falling on my head. "Mother, what's happening?" I said, and she answered, "For heaven sakes, it's raining!" A heavy downpour put the fire out, fifty feet from the woodpile. Mother swore she would never live in the woods again.

In the fall of 1942, mother and I saw smoke from Tall Timbers as the Ha Ha Tonka Castle burned down. Cousin John and his entire class watched from their school in Camdenton. Mother had taken me to Ha Ha Tonka a number of times to visit Mrs. Josephine Ellis who operated the hotel there for the Snyders. Mrs. Ellis was later remembered in interviews for making the most of the grand elegance of the place when she opened it for tours around 1937. I remember standing on a railing on the second floor and looking down into the great hall.

After that, Nat, Natalie Jr. and John moved to Warrensburg and were "Out of the Woods" forever.

The May 1998 *Rural Missouri* article describes the mansion in the words of Lillian Cunningham who was hired at 15 for housekeeping duties and to escort the visitors:

> I'd start the tour in the ballroom chatting with the group until it got big enough. All the rooms opened up off that room. There

Ha Ha Tonka Interior view of Main entry courtyard and staircase

were two huge living rooms across the front of the mansion. One was a music room of sorts, with an ornate baby grand. People often listened to music there. The dining room was divided from the great hall by huge pillars. A beautiful sun room was furnished in wicker with rose and sage cushions. Large arched windows with tiny leaded panes not only allowed the sun in but provided a beautiful view of the hillside overlooking the lake. From the dining room we went up the grand staircase to the bedrooms with massive four-poster beds and ornate furniture. After a successful year of tours, Josephine opened the hotel which would come to be known as "The Castle". Cooking the meals herself, with Lillian waiting tables, Josephine and I made a bit of profit until that spark flew out of one of the chimneys.

After moving back to Warrensburg The Captain had work to do back home and wouldn't need to dwell on the loss.

Once again she decided, Don't look back…. Onward!

Growing up fast at Tall Timbers and wearing her own little overalls, Natalie Jr. with her dog by a large woodpile. Wood in quantity near the log house would soon become a safety concern

Chapter Seventeen

NEEDED AT HOME

Nat Jr.'s account of her first pony was published in the 1999 Women's History Month Writing Project Collection created by the UCM Women's Consortium and Writing Across the Curriculum program.

Merry Legs and Mother
by Natalie Jr. Halpin

My Grandmother Wilson had a knack for naming things; HURRICANE HILL for the family home place, TALL TIMBERS, the log house and 70 acres belonging to her daughter and family in the Ozarks and my Shetland pony, MERRY LEGS.

Merry Legs first arrived in the back of an old Dodge pick-up truck. My Uncle John had loaded her out of a farmer's weed-infested pasture rescuing her from treatment either horrible or non-existent and brought her to the Court House Square in Camdenton. At the time, my father, Max Prussing, served as Presiding Judge [now called Commissioner]. While "Unk" went into the Court House to summon my father, the old timers gathered round the truck bed. In those days horse trailers were virtually unheard of. Merry Legs was behind wooden slats, known as stock rails. The old men of Camdenton made a habit of sitting under a shade tree on the Court House lawn. When this unusual four-legged animal appeared with shaggy mane and tail, tangled with cockleburs, mud caked coat and long forelock hiding her eyes, they pondered her origin.

"What could that be", one inquisitive old fellow asked.

"Don't know," another muttered.

By the time Unk and my Father appeared, there was quite a crowd. "What is that thing, "asked an old man with a beard.

My uncle answered, "A Siberian Yak." And so, Merry Legs also came to be known as "Yak".

After the fires near Tall Timbers, Grandmother Wilson became ill, and we moved back to Hurricane Hill.

Now that I was 5 years old, it was time for me to attend Miss Sweet's kindergarten class at the Laboratory School. The school was part of the college and was called the "Lab School" because it was just that. Young and non-traditional student

Nat Jr. moves to Hurricane Hill... figuring out life in town with her cousin John

teachers were put to the test and so were modern educational techniques at a semi-private small school on the campus where the students would be observed while "practice teaching."

As soon as we moved back to Warrensburg, mother made sure I had my pony. Merry Legs had a big pasture and a barn she shared with the family's Jersey milk cow. I was so happy to be allowed to ride Merry Legs to Kindergarten... all by myself. Each day I would ride up Clark Street.

Five blocks seemed a long way for a 5 year old to walk so it was decided that I could ride Merry Legs to school if I stayed on the sidewalk. Once at school, I tied her to the merry-go-round, making it easy to mount from the platform for my return home later in the day.

Everything went well for a week, until the day Mr. Carleton happened to be setting out the bottles at the back of his grocery store for the milk man [who then went from store to store picking up and delivering carriers full of reusable glass bottles. At one time, milk products were delivered right to your door at home, too.]. The door opened directly onto the sidewalk, and as I passed by he took one look at me and yelled, "Get that pony off my sidewalk! I've got customers walking by who don't want to step in horse manure. "

Well, tears came to my eyes and rolled down my cheeks as I turned Merry Legs toward home. If I couldn't ride by Mr. Carleton's, I couldn't go to school—certainly not on Merry Legs. My instructions were to stay on the sidewalk. When I got home and told my story, mother said, "Nat, for heaven's sake, ride your pony on the other side of the street."

Merry Legs was the beginning of my lifelong love of horses. When I outgrew her, she went to live with another family where she lived to be nearly 40 years old and was loved by many children. My mother's lesson, based on these early experiences with my pony, has stuck with me all of my life. "There's more than one way to skin a cat", as they say, and mother was very good at figuring out how to get around a situation that didn't please her. So, there's always more than one side to a street. Allowing me to ride Merry Legs for hours on end developed my passion for horses, but mother had an even more valuable gift to give—determination and persistence to get around any obstacle between me and my goals.

The most wonderful thing in all of this is that she taught me to be on my own and to take care of myself in any situation… She had all the confidence in the world that her kindergarten daughter would be fine riding Merry Legs at 5 and no qualms about sending me off to the University of Arizona in a car when I was 17. She and I both knew I was ready to take on the world.

Laura Francis
by Natalie Halpin

"Where's Emma? Where's Emma?" I asked. She hadn't been at Grandmother's house for three days now and I wanted to know where she was! Now that we had moved to Hurricane Hill, I had become very close to Emma. She was my cohort in many escapades. Emma is not coming back, was the answer I received.

Not coming back, what do you mean NOT COMING BACK? I yelled.

Emma is old and worn out like I am," Grandmother said. "A new lady is coming tomorrow. Her name is Laura Frances Collins."

"No, I want Emma!" I demanded.

Emma was the one I ran to when I skinned my knee, or hurt a finger. She was the one who took me beyond the garden to the chicken yard to watch while she chased that day's dinner around, catching it, and wringing its neck. She was the one who pulled my arm out of the new-fangled wringer washing machine when I stuck my fingers in the rollers. What would I do without the thin old black woman,

Laura Frances Collins, a new friend

with the friendly eyes that sparkled at me, with the bony fingers that tied my hair ribbons, and who whispered softly to me when I hurt myself? Why it was like taking away a favorite Aunt that I depended on. My mother was always attentive, but would say something like, "Nat, get up, brush off your skinned knee and get going." Emma would baby me, which I liked.

No one could replace her, or so I thought.

The next day Laura Frances came to the back door. I was sitting in the kitchen with Grandmother, waiting for her. My first observation was that she was young, so maybe she would move faster and play with me. She had a very pleasant smile as she looked down at me and said, "so you're little Nat." She had lots of hair, very thick and straight, so surely she could braid my hair with ribbons. Her nimble fingers looked like they would be good at plastering on band aids and such. Maybe it wouldn't be such a hard transition after all. When she fried the first chicken, served it with mashed potatoes, gravy and cherry pie for dessert, I knew everything would be all right.

At first, Laura Frances came five days a week, but she was raising two boys by herself so she needed better income than Grandmother could afford. After a few years, Laura Frances only came one or two days a week, while taking other jobs.

Her sons excelled in school. Both have led very successful and productive lives. Her thirteen grandchildren are all doing well, most if not all are college graduates.

Laura Frances taught me many things through the years. I learned to get along with others, no matter the color of their skin. I wish I could say that I had as many black friends as she had white ones. All who came in contact with her admired her. She taught me how to iron my clothes. This came in very handy when I went away to university and needed extra spending money. I could starch and iron collars and cuffs like a professional. I made many dollars ironing my well-to-do friends' designer dresses and their White Stag sportswear.

A leader in her church, Laura Frances served on many committees and she sang in the choir, often as the soloist. I knew and loved my friend for over 50 years. My only regret is that I never got to hear her sing. Now, I know that if I get to heaven, she is already there... singing with the angels. And I will at last get to hear her.

Camp Carry-On reunion, back on Hurricane Hill in Warrensburg

Chapter Eighteen

RISING TO THE CHALLENGE OF SOME TOUGH BREAKS

Little Nat's Broken Leg and Camp Greystone

In late December of 1945, just a few days after Christmas, Nat Jr. was planning on showing off her prized Christmas present—a metal wire basket for her bicycle. She set off for her best friend Patsy Fisher's house, just down the Hurricane Hill lane but she never got there. Patches of ice obstructed her way, and Nat and her bike went crashing to the ground. Her upper leg was badly broken and she was sent by ambulance to Children's Mercy Hospital in Kansas City, where she remained in traction for six weeks. Little Natalie's 8th Birthday was celebrated in the hospital. Big Nat slept in a trundle bed in the hospital room. Afterwards, a body cast was put on and remained for another 6 weeks, at which time she was transported to an upstairs bedroom in the Wilson family home on Hurricane Hill.

Food was brought up from the kitchen, sponge baths given and bedpans emptied in a daily routine which was quite an ordeal for all concerned. At one point it took three people to carry her to a local doctor for an x ray and he said, "Her left leg will be 1 -2 inches shorter than the right." Mother Nat's response, "No it will not!" Knowing so much about physical therapy, she made sure that Nat Jr. could go to a special camp to regain her strength and mobility.

With no Physical Therapy available locally, Big Nat wrote her cousin Edwin

Natalie was so happy and proud about the new basket she received for her bicycle for Christmas

Hanna. Kate Campbell, Elma's youngest sister was living in Warrensburg in 1897 when she traveled to Yellowstone with the Wilsons. She later married Perry Hanna of the same city, and they moved to Brookfield, Mo. and opened a laundry and dry cleaning business. Their only child Edwin spent nearly every summer with his cousins on Hurricane Hill. He received his degree in Electrical Engineer-

1947

CAMP GREYSTONE

TUXEDO, NORTH CAROLINA

Tuesday, July 1, to

Tuesday, August 26, 1947

MRS. VIRGINIA SEVIER HANNA
DIRECTOR

BOX 1662 ● SPARTANBURG, SOUTH CAROLINA

Member American Camping Association

Camp Greystone's brochure promised new experiences in nature, productive activities, and friendship. Happiness was promoted here, too!

ing from Georgia Tech in Atlanta. While there, he met a charming southern girl, who would become his wife, Virginia Sevier who was studying at Agnes Scott College in nearby Decatur. They married and moved to Spartanburg, S.C. near her family. Virginia's parents, Dr. Joseph Sevier and wife Edith, founded Camp Greystone for Girls in the mountains of North Carolina near Hendersonville in 1920. Dr. Sevier was an ordained Presbyterian minister. When he died in 1945, ownership passed to Virginia and her husband, Edwin. Edwin was familiar with Camp Carry-On when Nat asked if she could bring Natalie Jr. for the 2 month summer session, knowing the exercise and planned sports would have the 8 year old back to normal. The cost of the camp was $375 and since that was more than the Prussings could afford, she said she would come to camp as a counselor in exchange. An agreement was quickly reached, and preparations were made.

Finally on the designated day for "cast" removal by the family's local physician Dr. Johnson, his office called. The doctor had announced that he would be out of town for another week or more! Well, Big Nat wasn't going to wait one more day. She went to the wood shed, brought back a hand saw, some big clippers and a pair of pliers. She did not listen to the terrified protests as she carefully sawed the cast off. It took no time at all, but there was lots of yelling from Nat Jr.! The little one's body had plenty of room originally, but had ballooned up due a healthy growing girl lying flat in bed and all that home cooking! No scrapes or pinches, the cast was off without leaving a scratch.

At Greystone, Big Nat became the Wilderness counselor and spent many nights in a tent "fending off bears", as she put it. She gladly did all this for the wellbeing of her daughter and to ensure full rehabilitation from the bike accident. Captain Nat was chosen to take girls on overnight camping trips into the Smokey Mountains. At the end of the camp session, her recovered daughter had legs of equal length and no limp. Natalie Jr. attended the camp three years.

The same could not be said for Nat. Sr. who, if the reader remembers, still wore a brace from the broken ankle, which had been misdiagnosed by the New York City doctor. Big Nat always had a limp due to that ankle and her daughter asked in the late 1970s, "Mother, wasn't it devas-

Camp Greystone offered riding lessons. Nat Jr. in her mother's jodhpurs and boots and a borrowed jacket

tating not to be able to play your beloved sport — basketball?" Her reply came quickly, "Why? I didn't have to PLAY it, I was TEACHING it!"

To Max from his Daughter, Little Natalie Jr.
  (from Camp Greystone, Summer 1946):
    Dear Daddy, I am sorry I have not written you sooner, but I have been busy. Dude has gone to Niagra Falls. Thank you for your letter. I got a letter from Patsy yesterday. When you get me my horse please get me a cold [coal] black one with a stair [star] on his forehead. There is a real pretty horse down here. I go riding today and I am so glad. Please get me a jumping horse because I am not afraid and I will stick to it if you will only get me one. That's all for now. Write soon. Love, Nat

Natalie Jr. remembers her mother crying only twice. The first time was when Elma Wilson died, in January of 1947. Aunt Mary O. Shattuck and John Wilson took Elma to Hot Springs Arkansas to "take the waters." Grandma Wilson had not been feeling well, and Mary O. had been to Baden Baden in Germany among other healing spas and was a big believer in mineral baths. So, on Friday evening, January 24th, they left Warrensburg to take their mother to the baths hoping for relief.

The obituary of the much beloved Elma Wilson states "She had enjoyed the trip to the fullest and rested well on Saturday night, but early in the morning suffered a stroke." In a tragic turn of events, she was taken to the hospital and died there, so it was with great heartbreak that the news was received back on Hurricane Hill.

Nat had been her mother's caregiver since moving from Camdenton back to Hurricane Hill in 1943 with her daughter and her nephew, John Wilson. Max continued his work as Post Engineer at Fort Leonard Wood, so he moved from their

Elma Wilson, the perfect hostess, a champion of community service

beloved "Tall Timbers" to Base housing at the Fort, driving to Warrensburg on only weekends until his retirement in 1958. He returned immediately as the family gathered to mourn the loss of their beloved mother. Her influence was visible in the talents and accomplishments of each of her children, but she, too had been a driving force in the community.

Her 1947 obituary from the *Star Journal* reads "Born in Ohio, February 21, 1868, Mrs. Wilson came here as a young woman [with a career as a telegrapher]. She was married September 1, 1888 to John H. Wilson. They spent a few years of their married life in Lewiston, Idaho and in Muskogee, OK. … Mrs. Wilson was president of the Warrensburg Chapter of American War Mothers at the time of her death, having served as president for many years. She was a past state president, being elected the second president for the state after the organization was formed following the First World War. She had served in various official capacities in the state organization and until recent years was a regular attendant at state meetings. No less interest was displayed by Mrs. Wilson in work of the Episcopal Church. She had been president of the Women's Guild for 30 years, retiring from that office two years ago. A staunch Republican she had been a party worker throughout her life.

A woman of positive convictions, Mrs. Wilson was a leader in all activities in which she was interested, however, took no less interest in her home and family because of her varied activities. She entertained frequently and her home was a gathering place for her friends and those of her children."

The second time Nat Jr. saw tears in her mother's eyes was when Big Nat blamed herself for the death of her Jersey cow's calf. The two Nat's and young John (Dude) Wilson went mushroom hunting in an area not far from the Hurricane Hill house. The calf was tied to a tree while the cow was grazing nearby. When they returned, the calf had wrapped its rope around itself and the tree until it was strangled. That time, they all cried."

Big Nat once had a Hereford bull named "TV", because Nat Jr. and John had decided to use money allotted for a newly available television set in a more practical manner. They bought a bull. Perhaps they had heard the story about Nat's World's Fair Pig, or maybe the practical upbringing had carried over to another generation of Hurricane Hill residents.

TV the Bull, no nonsense Wilson/Prussing decision. Who needs a television anyhow?

Nat gets back into the livestock business, Polled Hereford cattle

Chapter Nineteen

GIRL SCOUTS AT HOME

Near Knob Noster, Missouri, just 10 miles, but a 30 minute drive from home, was the Knob Noster State Park, formerly the Montserrat National Recreation and Demonstration Area. It was the perfect location, with camp structures that had been built by the Civilian Conservation Corps after the Great Depression. It is not surprising that Captain Nat saw to it that Little Nat was a Girl Scout, and so to build upon that experience she created a camping program, in the woods, but a bit closer to her birthplace. From 1949 to 1952 Natalie Prussing was the Director of

Young Natalie holds what used to be very common, a paper cone used for drinking, the original paper cup as these girls gather for refreshment

Girl Scout Camp at Knob Noster State Park. Backward Glances in the *Daily Star Journal* noted that on June 5, 1949 the Warrensburg Girl Scouts were home from a week camping at Knob with Mrs. Max Prussing.

It is obvious that camping was very near and dear to the heart of our Captain Nat. After returning home from the Ozarks from 1949 -1952 Captain Nat taught a camping course at the same college where she started in elementary school. From the students in that class came counselors for the Girls Scout Camp she would establish and direct at Camp Bob White. A requirement to finish the course was to spend two weeks volunteering as a counselor. Staffing a group camp can be a daunting task, but with her connections Captain Nat persevered. Nat had been on the Girl Scout Council for many years and in 1949 she thought it was time to establish a regional Girl Scout camp at Knob Noster State Park. She wanted

Captain Nat watching over young campers in her favorite attire

it to be 2 sessions of a week at a very low cost for the girls. Three meals a day, plus outdoor cooking was included in the price. The cook would be the only paid staff. By recruiting mothers as the workers she kept the cost at 12.50/week per camper. The mothers felt privileged to be asked and most often said yes. The mothers washed dishes, set tables for dinner and moved them around for the cleaning between meals and for different uses of the building. They swept floors, hauled out the trash and completed other chores necessary to the running of a camp.

Camp included sports, swimming, arts and crafts, and outdoor skills. It allowed Nat to continue to promote the healthy outdoor lifestyle that was modeled at Dr. Sargent's camp in New Hampshire, almost 40 years earlier. She asked a local doctor's wife, Mrs. Virginia Maxon, a registered nurse, if she would be the Camp Nurse. Nurse Maxon gladly volunteered.

One prominent mother was asked to work washing dishes and performing other kitchen duties. Thirty years later, she told Natalie Jr, "I worked for two weeks in the kitchen which I never did at home, but you just didn't say "No" to your mother. Only she could talk me into washing dishes at scout camp when I had a maid at home and never had to wash a dish in my life!"

Not contented with only the group camp experience that had been facilitated by the State Park System, Nat presented plans to the Regional Girl Scout Council and then coordinated the building of the "Little House" in

Warrensburg, built back in the woods near the intersection of Business 50 (Young St.) and Warren in 1949. She presented the plan to the Regional Girl Scout Council and it was approved. The property was donated and Big Nat hired men to build. Max was helping on weekends home from Ft. Leonard Wood. The Little House was a two story building, 1,500 sq. ft., and was a great place for smaller individual troops of girls to have an overnight outdoor experience in a safe, but secluded location. Many a Girl Scout had wonderful

Captain Nat and two mothers who helped out.

memories of cooking, singing and sleeping in the loft designed for that purpose. Until the Little House closed recently, scouts rode the Amtrak and walked there for overnight campouts.

In 1987, the Mid-Continent Girl Scouts took part in the 75th Anniversary Celebration. The national organization chose 75 Women of Achievement who have achieved high standards of Girl Scouting and have attained excellence either professionally, or within their communities and families. Their selection represents the 52 million who have served Girl Scouting and have shared their values, beliefs and traditions. These women represent our organization's hope that all girls and young women become happy, thinking, caring and productive people. Captain Nat was named among those 75 special women.

Captain Nat and her volunteer Counselors at the Girl Scout Camp she organized at Knob Noster State Park

Chapter Twenty

MYRTLE GOODWIN

When a dear friend of Natalie Jr.'s passed away, she was asked to give a eulogy of sorts, documenting their friendship. She wrote the following and read it at the funeral.

"There she was, washing clothes using a wash board and ironing with sadirons heated on the kitchen wood stove. I walked into Grandmother's kitchen. Myrtle came over in a rush, picked me up in her big, strong hands and hugged me. She said, "My little Nat, with the snow white hair." We were quite a contrast, me, white as a lily and Myrtle, black as night. Since I had only seen one other colored person, I was fascinated by this black woman reaching out for me with such exuberance. I always hoped Myrtle would be helping out on the farm on my frequent visits and often she was there to greet me.

Myrtle and I were good friends from that very first encounter in my Grandmother Prussing's kitchen. I was maybe three years old, and she was about 50. Her husband Charlie, who was at least twenty years her senior, worked for my Grandfather for 40 years.

Myrtle Thompson Goodwin grew up in the Ozarks, in Benton County. She was born to Jake and Gertrude Thompson on December 30th, 1887, in a log cabin way back in the woods. She died on August 27th, 1996. Her father had been brought to Benton County from Kentucky as a slave, when he was seven years old. He had to take the name of the slave holder, as was often the custom. Myrtle moved to Warrensburg around 1910 and worked as

Quick Meal, the name of the stove used by the Prussings, would probably be considered slow today as it was wood or coal fired.

a domestic for many years, but if her employer did not treat her with respect, she quit on the spot. Myrtle was a liberated woman way before it was fashionable. She was a free spirit as well. "Myrtle takes care of Myrtle", and by being self sufficient she managed to make a little extra money by growing her own vegetables, raising chickens and selling eggs and milk.

Myrtle always had a cow and when her grass turned brown in late summer, my father would get a phone call. "Max, it's time for you to come and get my cow and take her to your farm for the winter." You didn't say no to Myrtle.

She built the clapboard house where she lived with her own hands. She had big gnarly working hands, strong, almost like a man's except— she had red polish on her nails when she died. You can tell a lot about a person by their hands. Old Charlie and she built that house on the west end of town and Myrtle kept adding to it. People were always giving her things and she kept them all. As a child, I would visit her with my Father. Once inside the house, I would follow him through a path from room to room until we found Myrtle in the back kitchen. On either side of the path her possessions were stacked high. I really never knew what most of them were because they were wrapped up. But she knew. Her mind never failed, even at the end.

At 106 she moved into a nursing home which was not to her liking, but for medical reasons it was decided best for Myrtle. On my visits there, we would talk about the good ol' days. You'd think she would have been bitter about her hard past, but no she was just matter-of-fact about it. She told me that the early years were lean. Her Mother had very little money to feed and clothe her children, but there were always pretty Sunday dresses for the girls. She said, "We had to walk two miles through the woods to get to church and when we returned home our white dresses would be black with ticks".

Myrtle's father died when she was only six years old, but she said she remembered him well. She had a large picture of him in an ornate frame hanging on the wall of her house. Myrtle was proud of her father, Jake Thompson, who was freed from slavery… to some extent and kept on working hard in Benton County until he died young. You could tell Myrtle resented the fact that her Father didn't even get to keep his own name when he was brought to Benton County by the slave owner who Myrtle still called "Ol Massa".

One day while visiting Myrtle at the nursing home, she said, "Nat, bring me some Indian Rocks, your Father used to find them along the creek at the farm." So, on my next visit, I dutifully took her three arrowheads. She quickly slipped them into her pocket. I asked her, "What are you going to do with those?" We were sitting on her bench at the elevator with others near. She said, "I can't tell you now, too many people will hear, I'll tell you later", but she never did.

Myrtle could really cook! She always had something cooking on her stove and during her reminiscing, she was talking about fruit pies. Our mutual friend, Laura Frances Collins was an outstanding cook especially when it came to pies. I said, "Cherry pie is my very favorite thing to eat and Laura Francis can bake the best cherry pies in the world." Myrtle said, "You haven't tasted mine."

That was Myrtle, confident and straight forward. Right up until the end of her long life, she commanded respect. There was a bench on which she sat every day at the nursing home, waiting to go down in the elevator for meals. People respected the fact that it was "her Bench". There are people who demand respect and there are people who earn respect. Myrtle earned it, and demanded it, too.

One time Myrtle telephoned me and said, "Nat, you go out and find some bittersweet root for me to boil." Bittersweet is a bushy vine bearing orange berries that is found along fencerows. I hunted and hunted and finally found some out on Bristle Ridge, a place Myrtle once lived. I took the bittersweet roots to Myrtle and asked, "After you boil them, what are you going to do, drink it, rub it on or what?"

She said, **"I can't tell you that or it won't take effect."** Whatever she did with it must have worked, she lived to be 108.

Chapter Twenty-One

THE WISDOM OF MAX PRUSSING

Possessions and Responsibilities
by Natalie Jr. Halpin, 1992

Natalie Halpin wrote: "Each added possession means an added re-sponsibility," my father said to me many times. I guess that is what he was thinking when he refused to buy "that worthless, God-forsaken property, around the Lake of the Ozarks, when he had the opportunity before all the development began.

Max Prussing and Ralph Vincent had a survey office in Linn Creek, the original county seat of Camden County. In the late 1920s, Union Electric of St. Louis bought surrounding property for the Lake of the Ozarks and hired Max and Ralph to be head surveyors of the Lake.

After Bagnell Dam was completed and the lake filled, many farm-ers, landowners and the whole town of Linn Creek sold out or stayed and watched the waters cover their land. Many Linn Creekers moved to the new county seat, which was named Camdenton. Max and Ralph moved their office to this new town.

The land around the Lake was cheap, dirt cheap. No one wanted those rocky hillsides. It was difficult if not impossible to dig a well. There were very few roads and no electricity. A few fishing camps with cabins appeared but fishermen were not coming to the area in droves. No, it was not considered good business sense to buy worthless land in the depression or even afterward, for that matter.

Ralph Vincent died in the 1970s, but his wife Lucille and I have kept in touch through the years. Even though I lived in Warrensburg and she in Camdenton, I visited her every year. Several years ago, on such a visit, we were discussing her husband's love of horses. She handed me a picture of Ralph on a big black Walking Horse. Lucille knew my long association with horses so we often spoke of my last trail rides.

I said, "Lucille, my horse trailer and truck are getting so old, I sure need better transportation, but I can't afford a new rig. If your husband Ralph, and my father had bought lake property, we would be millionaires today!"

"Ralph did!" said Lucille.

Nat Jr Grows & Sells Strawberries

A few days later, a mutual friend reported Lucille had recently sold a 200 acre parcel of land to a golf course developer for $2 million. As I shift my 1988 Ford truck into high gear, pulling my 1975 horse trailer, I just remember my Father's words, "each added possession means an added responsibility!"

That didn't keep Max from adding a few needed possessions here and there. Until he was no longer able, he took care of each item, each tool, each animal, each building, and knew his every acre, field and stream, as well as anyone could. The Prussing Farm, its home, outbuilding and barns are still under the vigilant care of his daughter, Natalie Jr. even though now property of the University.

Hurricane Hill, the home place, requires constant upkeep, too. Natalie Jr. lives in the home she built with Steve, her husband. Cousin John Wilson lives in the two-story home, and the lovingly built home of Max and Nat is shared with guests and friends. Max's lessons—and, perhaps more importantly, loving exposure to his careful and attentive way of work—were not lost on her. She cares for the tools and the buildings, as Max would have wished. Natalie Jr. serves as an example to university students who are willing to put in a good day's work. She employs skills that must be passed on to share with future generations. If not shared, the hard work and success of a century of farm families like hers may be lost, along with the agrarian lifestyle.

Max's responsibilities in his position at Ft. Leonard Wood are largely overlooked in histories that have been written today, but letters to increase his responsibilities and to recommend him for commendations or promotions speak for themselves.

By 1940 Max and Nat's beloved Ozarks were on the cusp of a momentous change almost as profound as the creation of the Lake of the Ozarks ten years previous. Again, Max Prussing was to play a pivotal and enduring role.

As tensions in Europe continued to escalate the decision was made in Washington to expand military infantry and engineer training to produce a combat-ready force. This prudent doctrine of preparedness had an advocate prior to World

John (Dude) Wilson and Natalie Prussing on their way to school with their dashing older cousin, Lem Shattuck

War I in the person of General Leonard Wood, a physician and Theodore Roosevelt's commanding officer in the Rough Riders during the Spanish-American War. On December 3, 1940 ground was broken for the construction of the 65,000 acre military installation that was to bear his name. The site, 40 miles southeast of Camdenton, had been contested with Iowa but the influence of Max's 129th Field Artillery compatriot Capt. Harry Truman, now Senator Harry Truman, was decisive in the selection of Missouri for the proposed base. Max was there from the beginning as the herculean task of creating roads, rail access and infrastructure followed by buildings and facilities culminated in a workforce of over 30,000 laboring in inhospitable conditions yet grateful to find employment in the aftermath of the Great Depression. In 1941 the project comprised the largest regular single payroll in the United States.

As the camp approached completion Max was appointed engineer, directly responsible for the supervision of almost 600 civilian personnel including 65 firefighters, 44 plumbers and steamfitters, 83 carpenters, 21 electricians, 51 boiler mechanics, 36 equipment operators, and 31 clerks. The installation used 2,410 train car loads of coal annually, the equivalent of 24 trains of 100 cars each.

HEADQUARTERS FIFTH ARMY
1660 EAST HYDE PARK BOULEVARD
CHICAGO 15, ILLINOIS

THE CHIEF OF STAFF   8 October 1948

Mr. Max Prussing
Post Engineer
Fort Leonard Wood, Missouri

Dear Mr. Prussing:

    I have just returned to Chicago and I
want to take this first opportunity to thank
you for taking care of us so well at Fort
Leonard Wood on Wednesday and Thursday. I
particularly appreciated your taking care of
transportation for us and seeing to it that
we got off as planned.

    You have a fine camp and it certainly re-
flected the good work you are putting into it.

    I am

        Sincerely,

        JAMES M. GAVIN
        Major General, GSC

Mr. Max Prussing
Post Engineer
Fort Leonard Wood, Missouri

Young 'Jumpin' Jim' Gavin, World War II Airborne Division, was the only U.S. Army Lieutenant General who made four combat jumps with his men.

OFFICE OF THE COMMANDING GENERAL
Headquarters, Fort Leonard Wood

Fort Leonard Wood, Missouri

ALWCG   21 June 1956

Mr. Max M. Prussing
Deputy Post Engineer
Fort Leonard Wood and
The United States Army Training Center, Engineer
Fort Leonard Wood, Missouri

Dear Mr. Prussing:

    Upon my departure for retirement, I want to tell you how very
much I appreciate the work you have done and are doing for this Post.
You have well earned the title by which most people know you of "Mr.
Fort Leonard Wood".

    I think you can take great pride in this Post as a whole since
you have seen it from its very beginning and have exerted very material influence on its development. You have furnished a continuity
of the Post Engineer's work throughout the entire period. We are
now entering a period of greater recognition for the Post and it is my
sincere hope that your health will permit you to remain during the
coming years. You, above all others, will be the man who had the greatest influence in the physical plant of this Post and the Army owes you
a debt of gratitude for what you have done.

    My very best wishes to you and my hope that you will continue for
some time to assist in the development of the Post.

                            Sincerely,

                            FRANK O. BOWMAN
                            Major General, USA
                            Commanding

Captain Nat on Royal Rex at age 82

Max's versatility and abilities made him the perfect choice for Post Engineer. He continued to serve in that position until 1958 earning him the sobriquet "Mr. Fort Leonard Wood", attested to in a letter of appreciation from Commanding General Frank O. Bowman who also wrote: "I think you can take great pride in this post as a whole since you have seen it from its very beginning and have exerted very material influence in its development. You, above all others, will be the man who had the greatest influence in the physical plant of this post and the Army owes you a debt of gratitude for what you have done. "

June 20, 1944 from James A. Person, Post Inspector General to Commanding Officer, Fort Leonard Wood, who concurred:

"In accordance with the provisions of Paragraph 12, Army Regulation 20-10, 3 September 1943, it is recommended that Mr. Max M. Prussing, Senior Engineer, Control Branch, Post Engineer, be commended for his outstanding service at Fort Leonard Wood, Missouri during the FY 1944 for the following achievement:

"His untiring effort in capably supervising the various Post Engineer activities, his acumen and sound judgement in helping solve many maintenance problems and maintaining the admiration of his associates since the establishment of the Fort."

Max riding Chief

To be specific about these responsibilities, The Post Engineer is responsible for coordinating and supplying:

Buildings and Structures: Maintenance and Repair of 4.1/4 million square ft. of Barracks and Quarters, equivalent to a city of 15 to 20 thousand. Mess halls, Chapel and Outdoor theatre, Service Club and Library, Recreation Buildings and Field House totaling ¾ million square feet, over 3 million square feet of Warehouse and Storage space, Hospitals, Training Fields, Rifle and Grenade Ranges, Lawns, Hangars, Airfields and even a mock Nazi village.

Besides that there were 275 miles of roads and 28 miles of railroad including a Trestle Bridge. Not to forget the coal, electricity and other utilities and services required to support that population.

Randolph Davis, a Fort Leonard Wood Engineer, and Max shared a house, together with their bird dogs, while on Base. During Quail Season Max brought his dog "Flak" and Randolph brought "Joe" to the Prussing Farm to flush out the birds for a weekend of hunting. The dogs worked well together and the whole family had a delicious feast at the end of the day. Max had a habit of snoring and if it got too loud, his beloved Flak would nudge him with his nose until he quit. Flak had his own Fort Leonard Wood "dog tag".

The Barn 1902-2017…

—a poem by Natalie Prussing Halpin

As I look at the Mule Barn, I wonder what it has seen and heard over its life span.

I weep and I laugh as I caress the oak beams that were raised in 1902 by the strength of men and mules, supervised by my paternal grandfather, George Prussing.

A century ago in rural Missouri, there were no cars, no electricity, no phones, no plumbing, no mail service.

Our barn stood as a grand structure, a symbol of a physical greatness, not needing or wanting modern convenience.

Natalie Jr. hopes that her father and his quiet, determined way of life will be a guide for future generations. After he passed, Natalie Jr. found a 1919 newspaper poem by Edgar A. Guest among the personal items in her father's keepsake trunk.

Character

He never rose to fame, never starred in any game.
Never made a lot of money men's attention to attract;
He had never won a prize of a noticeable size,
And the brilliance of glory was a charm he plainly lacked;
Men of state would pass him by and would never catch his eye,
None would ever read his value in the fashion of his coat.
In just this his worth is told; that his word was good as gold,
And there wasn't any banker but would gladly take his note.
He was not a great success, never mentioned in the press,
There were very few who knew him, but no one had ever heard,
Any hint of sin or shame being connected with his name
And no one, of him, had hinted that he ever broke his word.
He just toiled from day to day, in a calm and easy way
Never sought the hills of glory or the pomp and power of rank,
But he lived his whole life through in an honest way and true.
And whene'er he wanted money he could get if from a bank.
There may be in world success, greater thrills of happiness,
There may be compensation in the loud applause of fame,

But when all is said and done he life's best reward has won
Whose character is witnessed by an undishonored name.
Though he lives apart, alone, and is very little known
and the plaudits of the people, round about, he's never heard,
He can hold his head erect, for he owns the world's respect,
When men say it to his glory, that he never broke his word.

Natalie Halpin and her dear horse, Cricket

Chapter Twenty-Two

OH, THAT MARY T.!

Bichon and the Saloon Keeper
by Natalie Halpin

'Nat, I'm bored, let's go out.' It was Phillip on the phone, my long-time friend, home on summer break from college.

'I'm ready', I said. 'Two more weeks until I head back to the University of Arizona and Warrensburg is dead as a doornail!'

'I'll pick you up in 10 minutes.'

He arrived in his Father's big black chauffer driven Cadillac. Phillip was the eldest son of the Warrensburg banker, Edwin Houx. Verlon Grant, the chauffer, opened the car door for me and Phillip said, 'We're picking up Mary T. and going to Breeze Inn for a beer.'

Mary T. Patterson, fashionable through-out her life

'Sounds good to me!' I said, and jumped in.

Mary T. was a character, and she was worldly. Her Father was a re-tired Warrensburg physician and had sent his only daughter to a fin-ishing school in New York City. She had returned and married a local boy, but it didn't last. Mary T. wanted more than Warrensburg had to offer. They divorced and Mary T. left for New York to find excitement and fortune. It wasn't long before she was affiliated with Elizabeth Arden, the big beauty corporation. For several years, she had been the managing director of the posh Elizabeth Arden Salon in Paris, France.

She made yearly visits to see her aging parents and we were anxious to hear about Mary T.'s latest adventures.

We pulled up in front of the house, and Phillip went to the door to escort her to the black Caddy. He wanted to impress this worldly woman. Via the services of Verlon, she climbed in, and in after her jumped Bichon, her French poodle. Bichon sat like a person, upright beside her. 'He only understands French,' she said.

Breeze Inn, our destination, was at the south end of town. It was not the café a Parisian would expect, but the only place one could enjoy a cold beer on a hot August afternoon.

Bichon, Mary T., Phillip and I entered the foul smelling tavern. Gale, the saloon owner, had a black patch over one eye. Her build was big and husky and she had an equally big and husky voice. By all reports Gale had once been married to Casey Stengel, the famous baseball player.

Gale came charging forward. Was this bar owner, who had a reputation for selling beer to underage students, going to throw us out?

'No Dogs Allowed', she yelled. 'Get that dog out of here!'

Mary T. was aghast and replied, 'This is Bichon, he has been in all the finest restaurants in Paris.'

'I don't care what you call that dog, or where he's been, he's not coming in here.' Gale told us and escorted us out the door.

So much for having a cold beer on a hot August afternoon. "

Mary T. and the Spy
by Natalie Jr. Halpin

Mary T. Patterson was flamboyant, dramatic, fashionable and worldly. She grew up in Warrensbusrg, but left after tasting the delights of New York City, France and especially Paris. She was the Salon Director for Elizabeth Arden in Paris for many years. In the late 1950s she became director of four floors of the Elizabeth Arden headquarters on 5th Avenue in NYC. The next time Mary T. made an impression on me was in 1959 when I [Natalie Jr.] went to New York to further my education after attending University of Arizona. Tobe-Coburn Fashion Merchandising School on Madison Avenue was my destination. Mother had written Mary T. for advice on the selection of a residential hotel for women. There were three on the school-approved list.

Mary T. wrote back: "There is only one place for Natalie to reside and that is the Barbizon Hotel for Women on 63rd and Lexington Avenue. Oscar is the doorman. He is very selective with whom he lets into the lobby to visit hotel guests. He has made quite a name for himself over the years."

So, off I went to New York, Tobe-Coburn, The Barbizon Hotel and Oscar. Everything was as new and exciting as a 20 year old could possibly imagine. The first weekend after my arrival, Mary T. invited me to dinner. I was looking forward to seeing her grand apartment which she had reported to her Warrensburg friends, had a view of Central Park.

When I arrived Mary T. said, "I have invited my friend for cocktails, he is a Russian spy." I couldn't believe my ears. But knowing Mary T. for many years, I had heard her fabulous stories of her Parisian friends; Countess this and Count that, with a Princess mentioned here and there. Now, a Russian Spy!

A knock was heard at the door. Mary T. opened it and said, "This is Nicholai Peshkova, he is with the Russian delegation at the U.N., and this Nicholai, is Natalie Prussing."

The distinguished, mustached Russian took my hand, kissed it, and said, " Natalia, it is such an honor to meet such a beautiful woman." I thought to myself, "this spy isn't half bad." We drank Vodka cocktails from fluted crystal glasses. After an hour of lively conversation, between them, I couldn't understand through his accent, he left.

Mary T. served a three course dinner, starting with an unfamiliar looking first course. "This is an endive salad, my dear, the rage of Paris." All I remember is, it was curly and crunchy. Then, the main course was something equally unfamiliar, but hesitating to enquire, I ate the tasty dish which was prepared in a heavy sauce. "I'm so glad you liked that", she said, "it was calf's tongue."

"Ugh, I thought!" Fortunately, I recognized the dessert, strawberries and ice cream.

Remembering Mary T.'s remarks about viewing Central Park from her window, I asked, "Where's your view of the Park?"

She said, "Oh darling, you can get a peek when you are sitting on the loo in the bathroom."

Later, I sat, and I saw.

It was an evening I will always remember: Cocktails with the Russian Spy, endive and tongue, and a view from the loo!

Chapter Twenty-Three
COMMUNITY INVOLVEMENT

In the fall of 1955, Nat Jr. left for the University of Arizona–Tucson. That left Big Nat with time on her hands, even though she was running the Prussing Farm, 5 miles east of Warrensburg. It was there, in 1952, she had established a purebred Polled Hereford herd of cattle. She was also looking after the needs of Max's mother, father and sister who all lived on the home place. At this time Max was the Base Engineer at Fort Leonard Wood military base, returning home on weekends until his retirement.

Later, he would run his family's farm business full time. His sister Leah Pearl was still living there and was a Weather Reporter.

At the moment though, Big Nat was ready for a challenge—that's what kept her engines roaring. That something was community involvement.

Politics
by Natalie Jr. Halpin

Johnson County had long been run by Democrats and Big Nat wanted to change the "Old Guard", the officials in the Courthouse. The organizational skills that she had been building during a lifetime in education, indoors and out, helped her to create/revitalize the Republican party of Johnson County to promote change. She was good at recruiting qualified candidates for office and the volunteers enjoyed working with her. By the early 1960s, Republicans dominated the Court House. She served as Johnson County Republican Women's Club president for a number of years. Nat also was chair of the Johnson County Republican Central Committee for many years. She was an alternate delegate to the Republican National Convention in 1960.

Through years of elections and politicking she saw wins and losses for the candidates she had groomed and promoted. When a candidate

Nat's overwhelmed being recognized by the Republican Women. At left, Suzie Nichols

lost her reaction was always the same. "We'll work harder and next time we will win." Failure was not in her vocabulary. She lived the life of encouragement, support and strength. Nothing got her down. She was always optimistic and never fearful. Her determination built a very strong Republican base in the county, which is still evident in 2017.

Excerpts from an Article from the *Warrensburg Daily Star Journal*... "Republicans Honor Mrs. Prussing" 2/13/79

On her 86th birthday, Natalie Prussing received a plaque naming her the "Grand 'Young' Lady" of the Grand Old Party at the Johnson County Republican Central Committee's Lincoln Day Dinner. In her own words, she was "looking for something to do. My husband had gone down to Fort Leonard Wood to lay out the fort, but I had to come back to Warrensburg to our farm because my father had died. I've always had some activity or interest, but I never thought it would be in politics. When I came into the party there were no Republicans in the county courthouse. But in 10 years, we had six out of the eight offices."

From 1958-1968 Natalie Prussing served as the Johnson County, Missouri Republican Central Committee Chair and from 1964-68 she was President of the Johnson County Republican Women's Club.

As Chairman of the Johnson County Republican Party, Nat was well-known, both in Jefferson City and among the politically inclined as a leader of the party faithful. About the time Jack Danforth, Republican became Missouri's Attorney

Nat met Vice-President Richard M. Nixon in 1960

General, his wife Sally published a cookbook. She sent one to Nat with the following note: "Mrs. Prussing, Many thanks for all your help to Jack. Best always, Sally D."

Her first political awareness came early, while her father was operating the Wilson's Clothing Store. He was elected mayor around the turn of the century presiding over the laying of the first brick paved streets. When she returned to Warrensburg she took charge of a loosely organized G.O.P. base and stimulated the growth of a political powerhouse. A closing thought from Nat, recalling a life of public service and education, "I've been very lucky."

Max used his extra time after retirement to build additions on the little white house, doubling the size of their home. In 1958 when Max remodeled, adding a large kitchen to their house, his wife requested a greenhouse with French doors that opened off the kitchen on the south side of the house. Another set of French doors would open into the living room, providing an inviting tropical view from many angles all year long.

Nat's dear friend, Clair Christopher had a greenhouse attached to her residence on South Street. Clair had two sisters, Marion and Maude. Maude taught Botany at CMS. The three Christopher girls had developed an heirloom tomato called "Sams", a family surname. The tomato was very popular, but when the ladies died, that special variety went with them. Big Nat fashioned her greenhouse after Clair's and Max built the structure that is still in use and in bloom with some of the plants that have been there for 60 years. Three different bougainvillea vines, a showy tropical plant, are a sight to behold, usually blooming in the middle of winter. Nat's green thumb lives on in those brilliant trees and the care that Natalie Halpin still bestows on the plants in the beautiful glass structure.

Inside Nat's greenhouse

Nat and Max's house on Hurricane Hill

Chapter Twenty-Four
NATALIE JR. MEETS AN FBI AGENT...

When Nat Jr. left the University of Arizona in 1959, she entered Tobé-Coburn School for Fashion Careers in New York City. Then she interned at Saks Fifth Ave. and Federated Department Stores Buying Office. Her first job was with Gimble's Department Store, the rival of Macy's, both located in the hub of downtown NYC in Herald Square. She was an assistant buyer. Then she moved on To Peck and Peck's buying office where she was an assistant buyer for their 78 stores across the U.S.

While in New York, she met a dashing F.B.I. Agent Steve Halpin.

Steve Halpin, investigating the Mississippi Burnings

They married in Warrensburg, June 9, 1961. Steve had been a P–47 Pilot in WWII. After the war he finished his degree in a year at the University of Minnesota, and then joined the F.B.I. as a special agent. In NYC he was assigned to the Organized Crime squad (anti-Mafia) and had many interesting cases. In 1961 the tensions and civil rights violations were intense in the South and Steve Halpin was assigned to the Atlanta, Georgia office. One of his civil rights cases, in 1964, was famously known as "Mississippi Burning". Three civil rights workers were missing and later found dead and buried in a dam near Philadelphia, MS. Steve was on the case for four months and arrested Deputy Sheriff Cecil Price. Eventually 19 men, all Ku Klux Klan members, were arrested. Another notorious case

Natalie Prussing Halpin, looking fashionable

Steve Halpin, F.B.I., in Columbus Circle, New York City

he worked was the kidnapping of Barbara Mackle. She was a student at Emory University in Decatur, a suburb of Atlanta. Suffering with Asian flu and staying in a hotel with her mother, Barbara answered a loud knocking on the door. A man, impersonating a police officer forced his way in the room and kidnapped Barbara. He buried her in a fiberglass box outfitted with an air pump. Gary Krist and his girlfriend demanded $500,000 ransom from Barbara's father, a wealthy Florida land developer. The chase went from Atlanta to Florida. Barbara was finally discovered in the Box 83 hours later-- alive, near Atlanta. The book "83 Hours 'Til Dawn" and the ABC TV story in 1972 "The Longest Night" recount the frantic tale of finding Barbara Mackle and apprehending Krist and his girlfriend.

During the 9 years in Atlanta, Nat Jr. was a Fashion Buyer for Rich's Department Stores. Rich's was not only the leading store in the South, but the largest. It was an "institution". Nat flew to NYC nearly every month for 4 or 5 days on buying trips and to California once a year.

Steve retired in 1970 and they moved back to Warrensburg, building their home on Hurricane Hill. Natalie Jr. knew she would be taking care of her parents when the time came and taking over the operation of the Prussing Farm. The fast pace and excitement of the big cities had come to an end. Nat Jr. took off her high heels and pearls and replaced them with cowboy boots, spurs and a bandana with absolutely No Regrets!

My First Tennis Dress or How to Get Your Man by Natalie Prussing Halpin. Published *in Living off the Land-A Gathering of Writings*, published 2004 by Dr. Robert C. Jones and the Warrensburg Writer's Circle.

'Twenty Dollars for a tennis dress?' I couldn't believe the salesclerk at Lord and Taylor.

The year was 1959 and I had been invited by my future husband, Steve, to play at the Forest Hills Tennis Club in Jackson Heights, NY. In those days, dressing for tennis was not a simple matter of shorts, a top and tennis shoes. "Tennis Dress" was a one-piece dress, white, with matching socks and tennis shoes.

Very few shops carried tennis apparel. Lord and Taylor was my only choice, and the investment represented twenty-five percent of my $100 a week salary as an assistant buyer at Gimble's Department Store in New York City. But I wanted to keep this date, even if it meant semi-starving myself for a couple of weeks. Twenty-five cent tuna sandwiches at Chock Full o' Nuts would suffice for lunch and cottage cheese, salad and an apple for supper. I could manage.

I'll take the dress, I said and carried it back to the one-bedroom studio apartment that I shared with Cheryl and Corinne, all of us recent graduates of the Tobé-Coburn School of Fashion Careers in Manhattan. The bedroom was a little cramped, to say the least—three single beds in a row, heads against the far wall, no space in between, but

Tennis Dress that snared a husband for Nat. Jr. even through her discomfort at first wearing

Natalie Jr. and Steve, ca. 1970

perfectly accessible by crawling in from the foot of the beds. We thought we were living in style: a second story apartment with a doorman; but no air conditioning!

When I modeled my new Lord and Taylor dress, Cheryl pointed out, "It's a little snug. A long-line bra might take care of that little bulge in the middle."

"You can borrow my rubber Playtex girdle [serious Spanx]," offered Corinne.

Nat Jr. and Steve, Orlando, 1992

With Corinne's girdle and a 'Slenderella' bra—another 5% of my salary, I was ready for Forest Hills.

The front of the club had a huge striped canopy covering the walk and entrance. Steve and I walked into the lobby—very grand with its walnut paneling

'We are happy to have you as Mr. Halpin's guest,' The receptionist said. 'Your locker room is to the right.'

I entered the locker room wondering how I was going to struggle into all my constricting garments without putting on a contortionist exhibition. I took one look at the posh pink and white décor and re-treated into a private shower stall. 'I always take a shower before a ten-nis match,' I announced silently—to whoever might be watching.

'Match', however, is not quite what it turned out to be. Every time Steve said, 'Just reach back and follow through on the ball', that longline bra gave me an agonizing pinch. I could hardly keep the tears back—let alone 'reach back'.

When Steve coached, 'Run. Move your feet!' that Playtex girdle didn't move—it just dug right in.

From that day forward, Steve probably knew that I would never make a tennis player. The dress must have fitted the occasion, however, because six months later Steve asked me to marry him. But never again did he ask me to play tennis at the Forest Hills Tennis Club.

The Lord and Taylor dress still hangs in the back closet, alongside my wedding dress—both yellow with time. To fit into either of those memo-ries, I am afraid it would take more than help from Slenderella or Playtex.

Chapter Twenty-Five

THE WISDOM OF
NAT WILSON PRUSSING

"Eventually things will work out one way or another; just make the best of it and keep going"

Nat always said, " If you have Lemons, Make Lemonade"

Natalie contracted tuberculosis and was confined to her room in the family home for a year. Because the Wilson's were a family of "doers", as they called themselves, she thought it would be a good time to take up quilting. Her father built her a frame and her mother provided the patterns and materials. What an accomplished quilter she became! Her pieces of art have been beautifully preserved and have been admired by friends and even a quilter's group. She totally recovered because of good food and good family care—at a safe enough distance to prevent infection of others.

Municipal Memory – with Intermission
by Natalie Jr. Halpin
Published in *K.C. Star Magazine*- May 14, 2000

"A trip to 'the City' was always a special treat. My family lived in Warrensburg, Missouri., and for special occasions we would drive the 50 miles to Kansas City. One such outing was in the late 1940s.

My cousin John [Wilson] and I had been given tickets to the Ice Capades at Municipal Auditorium in downtown K.C. John was 10 years old and I was 8 and we were on our own. That is, my mother and aunt dropped us off in front of the marquee and we were to meet them after the performance in the lobby of the Muehlbach Hotel.

Dressed in our best outfits, we were ushered to our seats. The performance was better than anything we could have imagined. The skaters sailed over the ice in glittering costumes. They jumped in the air, twirled and performed unbelievable feats. John and I sat on the edge of our seats… And then it was over! We were so disap-

John Wilson and Nat Jr, about the time they had fun at the Ice Capades in Kansas City

pointed, it had been so short. We left the grand marble halls and walked the three blocks to the Muehlbach. Once in the lobby, we sat and sat. Finally my mother and aunt arrived and inquired how long we had been waiting. After telling them we had been there for an hour, they exclaimed, "You left at the intermission!" How were two kids from Warrensburg supposed to know about intermissions?!"

In 1949, the Warrensburg Saddle and Bridle Club was organized and both Nats were charter members. Our horses were generally kept out at the Prussing Farm while a cow was kept in town for milk. Milking was always done in the barn. When organized rides were first held by the Saddle and Bridle Club the club ring was located in a field which was in the parking lot just north of the McDonald's on Business 50. Mother and I would ride the horses in from the farm on the evening before the Club Ride.

No More Phone Calls
by Natalie Jr. Halpin

In 1955 at 17, Natalie Jr. entered the University of Arizona in Tucson, as a freshman. All freshmen were invited to attend a Bonfire on "A" Mountain. In a line of traffic driving a bright red used

Pontiac (or "dirty Red Streak" as it was referred to) the group left in a procession for the event. A quick stop was made by the car in front of her, she stopped in time, but the next car in line hit the Pontiac, doing enough damage to end Natalie's trip. Knowing what to do, because of her upbringing as a self-sufficient individual, she told her friends to get rides with others who came along while she waited for the police and called the insurance company. Now, too late to make the bonfire, Nat Jr. returned to her dorm to call home and report the incident before Big Nat got a report from the Insurance Company. At this time using "long distance" telephone services might have cost $5 or so… quite a lot of money at the time, you might have paid your electric bill….After listening patiently to the dramatic retelling of the incident, Nat Sr. said, "You could have said this with a 3 cent stamp!" Fortunately, in the years to come, many letters were written home, but NO MORE PHONE CALLS.

In 1970, Natalie Jr. left her life in the fashion industry and her F.B.I. agent husband Steve retired from service. They moved from Atlanta to Hurricane Hill. The house they built there on the family hill made three generations of the Wilsons who would grow up on that lovely parcel of land. That piece was first purchased before the Civil War by Mr. Zoll, whose name is honored in the street off which the Hurricane Hill lane leads. Some of the Wilsons would set roots in other states and only return, some with children, to visit the scene of so many lovely memories. Others, most notably Natalie Jr., would return after groundbreaking careers and pick up farming and loving the land, being good stewards of it, wanting to preserve the hard work of their predecessors, for the purpose of educating young people, now and in the future. All were touched and enlightened by the straight forward wisdom of Captain Nat.

In the early 1970s, Big Nat was diagnosed with breast cancer. She had a total mastectomy in Kansas City and upon her return to the doctor's office, a blood test was taken. In a grave voice, she heard the doctor say she had leukemia. She said, "Hell, I don't have leukemia!" The next time her blood was tested. No Leukemia!

Nat Wilson Prussing had never been back to San Antonio, Texas since she left her job as administrator of Physical Education to return to Missouri. She had a desire to see San Antonio and the surrounding Hill Country . Nat's one time beau, Frank Pancoast, a banker had been

Nat Wilson Prussing, best shot in Texas!

her beau for a time and in 1922 had given her a gift of a beautiful painting of Bluebonnet Fields of Texas by Julian Onderdonk. This signature work was featured with Nat Jr. on Antiques Road Show-Kansas City filmed in August of 2013, broadcast in 2014.

In April of 1977 sisters Gladys Anderson Pole and Carolyn Anderson accompanied Big Nat and Little Nat to revisit San Antonio during the Blue Bonnet Festival. Gladys had been the Supervisor of Art in the district during Nat's tenure.

The hotel in which they stayed was a lovely old building on the Rio Grande that had once been a dental college, converted by then into a grand hotel. Natalie Jr. went to the phone book and found Frank Pancoast! She proceeded to dial the number under protests from her mother. An elderly woman's weak voice answered " Helloooo". Natalie Jr. inquired about Frank..... After learning she was speaking to Frank Pan-

1977, Captain Nat revisited old stomping grounds among the bluebonnets of Texas

coast's widow, and that he had passed away several years before, Natalie Jr. identified herself and her reason for calling.

His widow said, "Nat Wilson!!! Frank always said she was the best shot in Texas!"

Frank and Nat loved hunting and target practice and had spent many hours in the big out-of-doors in Texas. During that trip in 1977, the Bluebonnets were in full bloom as if to say, "We've been waiting for you to return."

Natalie Jr asked her mother at age 86 why she hadn't married Frank Pancoast and she

1977, Max on Royal Rex

replied, "I wasn't going to spend the rest of MY life in Texas!"

Upon the 100th anniversary of Sargent College in 1981 (by this time a part of Boston University) Natalie received word in separate letters that she had earned two different Distinguished Alumni awards. She had "three years in Theory and Practice in Physical Education including a one month course in field and water sports". Recognized for putting the philosophy of Dr. Sargent and his college to work during a long and honorable career as a Physical Education pioneer, Nat received the *Sargent Spirit Award* and was inducted into the *Twinness Society*.

Unable to attend the awards ceremony at Sargent, Nat sent the following note:

"What a surprise to receive the Twinness Membership Award. I was flattered to think I would be cited for this award. Because of my health, I cannot attend, but cannot think of anything I'd rather do than be there for this event. Would really like to see some of my old classmates who put me through the ropes as a freshman. Like—combing my hair in pigtails all over my head and tying them in twine and having to wear it that way for a week, to say nothing of trying to dunk me in the swim pool, but It backfired as one of them got a dowsing instead of me! I'd like to be there to have another laugh as I laughed then.

I would appreciate a copy of the others honored, especially if any are of my vintage. Eighty-eight, instead of the eighty-seven my daughter so flatteringly wrote. It's the first time I have had my life flashed in front of me, and I'm a bit embarrassed by it all, but very flattered."

Upon learning of a second award she wrote again: "The Sargent Award has again overwhelmed me. I felt it enough to receive the Twinness and now this! I would certainly like to be present that day to receive the award, but due to failing health, it is impossible. The feet won't move in the right direction at the right momentum—not like the good ol' days when leaping in the air to make a basket was so simple. "Getting old is Hell". I keep fighting it every step of the way at 87. I'm still fighting. Sargent brings back such wonderful memories it seems like yesterday! My regards to you on this grand Centennial occasion."

The same year—she would have been 87—she was still fixing the family vehicles. But , she lamented, "I am just getting so damned old. They won't let me drive anymore."

For her remaining years, Captain Nat enjoyed life at the little white house that Max had built on Hurricane Hill. She never stopped working. Besides politics, her later years were filled with new friends and more outdoor experiences.

She was in her last decade when Big Nat wanted a cat and answered an ad in the newspaper for a 'free kitty'. Not only was she getting elderly, but was also a bit unsteady on her feet. The kitty was constantly underfoot, and in her concerned daughter's mind, it was only a matter of time before that cat would cause a fall. Natalie Jr. took matters into her own hands and gave away the menace.

The next day her mother was again looking through the want ads. The handwriting was on the wall, so Natalie Jr. rushed to the animal shelter and selected a new, more appropriate kitty. She became known as 'Kat with a K' and was a distant companion to the aging Nat, only intruding into her space by sleeping on the foot of the bed, keeping her toes warm.

After years of heartfelt work and play, traveling the country and the world more than most of her contemporaries, Nat left for a different kind of journey at her passing, October 25, 1986.

A friend of both Nat's, Bernice Craig delivered this writing at her funeral:

"Once, thirty years ago, when I was sore oppressed by the critical illness of my husband, Nat Prussing came to my door. Energetically she informed me that she had brought me a shrub from Hurricane Hill and

Kat with a K in 1995

had brought her nephew to plant it. That smoke tree stands today 20 ft tall on my lawn, a living memory of the graciousness of Natalie Prussing.

The words that follow were written by Nat Jr.:

Natalie Wilson Prussing loved the beauty of nature. Her green thumb was revealed in the flowers in her greenhouse and yard. She marveled at the calves on her farm and always called everyone's attention to the birds at the bird feeders and the colorful trees. She was in love with life and its surroundings. There was meaning in every aspect of her life. She didn't just wander aimlessly through… she left her mark here and there along the way. Many girls who attended her "Camp Carry-On" in the Ozarks, her students of P.E. and camp counseling at the various institutions in which she taught, were inspired by her enthusiastic teachings and her knowledge. She inspired many with her political and patriotic beliefs. She was an optimistic backer of many causes. Defeat was not in her vocabulary – There was always tomorrow if today was not up to expectations.

What a marvel! To be always enthusiastic, loving, gracious, determined and happy, Nat inspired those she knew with courage and strength.

Max, 93, followed her October 10, 1989

They both tried to leave the world a better place than they found it, touching many lives along the way. The letters and tributes that follow, pay great testament to the impact they had on each person's life they touched. Their daughter continues on that path. She, too, has touched the lives of many, and her guiding way is well illustrated in the following writing…

Watermelon with Natty
by Janelle Cammack

A memory of Natalie Jr. in the eyes of a young girl, in retrospect, from the daughter of her friend Judy Cammack. It was written in 1998.

The honk of the old blue truck and the howlin' of the latest dog sounded her arrival. She was often runnin' early, and I was always ready, not wantin' to miss a second. I knew without seein' her she'd have on her red bandana, have her watermelon cuttin' pocket knife in its usual place and smell a little bit like mothballs. My friend, Natty, was predictable like that.

I wanted to be a farm girl somethin' fierce, but my family lived in town. The biggest animal I was allowed to keep in the back yard was a beagle named Daisy. Life just didn't seem fair 'cause of that.

Life changed for me when I met Nat. I knew instantly I wanted to keep her around more than any stray I'd ever come across. She was the horse-craziest grown-up I'd met! In fact, I think she liked horses as much as I did. I'm not sure if she pretended to be ridin' while lookin' out of the car window, but if I had to bet on it, I'd say yes! I think she was fond of me from the beginnin' too. I knew she liked me as soon as I smiled, 'cause I looked pretty close to a horse as any kid could with my unusually big teeth in my eight year old head.

Max would already be there, no matter what time of day it was. The workshed would smell of the fire he tended, and the leather he was workin', makin' soft in his old, worn hands. Chiefy would be ready too…nayin', tossin' his mane, and carryin' on as I jumped from the truck.

The race was on… Tack, brush out, halter on, hooves cleaned, bridle in place, and finally—the saddle. Nat still had to help me with that part. She told me the tales of that saddle, how it had been used in the war by her father, My Max, I called him. Then how his hands had worked it so that it could be used by me. I knew that saddle was pretty special, so I must be special too.

Janelle Cammack and her beloved Chief

When in that saddle, I felt I was part of the Cavalry, ridin' to warn my men, instead of just lookin' for new baby calves. I'd forget all my pretendin' when I'd see that new white face peek up at me from the tall grass, eyes as big as the sky, fringed with the prettiest lashes I ever saw. Natalie let me help her tag ears, and spray for flies. I wasn't even one of the hired farm boys—No, Natalie said I was more like 'family'.

Family is real important to Natty. The farm had been theirs for years. Everybody was kinda connected to it, she said.

Natalie's mom, Big Nat didn't come out much anymore, but she didn't like to miss out on picnic days on the farm. Even my mom would put on her sunscreen and come too if there weren't too many bugs around that day. Then we were kinda connected, too, I decided. On those days, the four of us rode to our picnic spot in the truck, not bouncin' up and down too much on account of bein' so crammed in there. We trudged through the cherished pasture, then we'd feast under the big oak by the pond.

Quieter picnics were the ones Natty and I took on horseback. Me on the trustworthy Quarter Horse Chiefy, who never could get enough clover, and Natalie on the regal jumper, Cricket. We'd find a spot, any spot, and make our picnic. Sometimes we'd just have pears and apples from the cluster of fruit trees by the white farm house. Always, Nat would pull out her knife and slice them for us. It bothered me a lot at first 'cause I'd seen her use that knife earlier in the day to cut the twine off of the hay bale we threw to the horses, or cut a piece of leather… I never said much, that was just the farm way, I figured.

One day, Natty told me she had a surprise for me down in the garden. Max toiled out there on his good days, plantin' an' weedin', lookin' and hopin'. On that particular day we were sent to discover if the watermelon were ripe. Natty jumped from her horse and I was given the duty of holdin' her reins, and keepin' my horse from eatin' everything that was growin'. With much anticipation and thumpin', Natty found the perfect melon. It squirted sweet juices

Nat caning chairs

from the first cut. She handed me the wedge, and I buried my face in the pink fruit. I was covered with sticky wetness from my chin to my boots—smilin' all the while.

It remains one of my greatest memories—enjoyin' my two favorite things in the world at the same time, watermelon and horseback ridin'. Well, I guess three favorite things, 'cause I can't forget to count Natty!

Several Carry-On campers wrote to Nat on her 90th Birthday to wish her well. Helen Schmid Hardy wrote from California remembering, "thanking you for happy years at Carry-On… If only I could tell you how much those camping years meant to me… the influence you and Geneva had on my life. To this very day, I could sing every song on the Music sheet…even break into song on occasion."

Libby Siegmund Conrad wrote from Ft. Myers Florida: "I walk every day and often need to sing our old CCO hiking song to get me going, 'Onward and Up we march along—' Enjoy your special day, Love always.

Max and Nat

Act IV
THE LEGACY OF
MAX AND NAT

AFTERWORD
Recollections of Family and Friends

Mrs. Stephen Halpin, 1300 Briar Cliff Road, Atlanta, GA
2/12/1969
Dear Mother,

This is your 75th birthday, I hope you have a happy day and at least 25 more happy ones. I thought it a good time, on your birthday, to tell you "What my Mother means to me." I think the last time I wrote it down to you was when I was in the 2nd or 3rd grade. Do you remember that homemade card? Think it's in my dresser drawer still.

You were everything to me as a kid and when I look back, I wonder how you did it all. You were a playmate, teacher, and mother. Think of all the beautiful days we spent at Tall Timbers, which I remember vividly, such as playing "bird" on the tricycle, sliding down the make-shift slide on Daddy's knee, setting off fireworks or watching them sparkling off the white fence, drinking warm milk from Tom's cow, insisting on spooning up the bantam hen's broken egg, playing in a huge sand pile behind the garage, crying from the smoke of the forest fire, trying to walk across the cattle guard, sledding on the pond across the highway, feeding Tug Boat and on and on and on and on…

Thank you mother for making me such a happy child. You made me a happy grownup because of all the love and attention you have given me. And think of the wonderful times I had riding horseback with you and Daddy. That farm was a wondrous place for me—I thought, and still do, Daddy "King of the World." I followed him around like a shadow.

And didn't we have fun with all the camping? My, I was proud that MY Mother was the camp director at Scout Camp and everyone was so envious. And our trip and summer at Greystone. The hardest trip for you must have been the one to Colorado when you took

The family that travels together, never unravels

Martha and me—nothing like "terrible teenagers." I must have been positively horrible and I hope you long ago forgave me for being age 12 through 17.

I just know, Mother and Daddy, you both were the best parents in the world when I was growing up and I love you very much and appreciate all you've done for me and given me.

So, Mother, please promise you'll have lots more Happy Birthdays, I need for you to be around for lots more years. I must have my Mother and Daddy to come home to once in awhile.

Love, Nat

Letter from John Wilson, 505 Hurricane Hill, Warrensburg, MO
April 2017

Aunt 'Nat,' my father's youngest sister was important to my upbringing. She and Uncle Max had readily agreed to take me in to stay with them in their Ozarks home in 1942 when I was 6 years old and in the first grade. It was at the end of the Great Depression and at the beginning of the Second World War. My dad had brought me back from California that year to live with them and with their young daughter, Nat Junior, because my mother died and my dad was seeking new employment in the rapidly growing defense industry.

John Wilson and Gwen Innes, 1991

John Wilson and Natalie Prussing Halpin, on Hurricane Hill 2017

What strong and caring people my aunt and uncle were. I always felt treated and loved as a full member of their family. A year later we had all moved to the family home in Warrensburg to join my father and other family members.

Aunt Nat was knowledgeable about most everything, particularly those practical skills we all need to best grow and thrive. From health-care to education to sports, business, farming, community activity, child rearing--you name it, she was always a doer. If you were to ask my favorite memory of Aunt Nat, or of my Uncle Max, it would be hard to come up with one. I have thousands of memories, all good ones. My Aunt and Uncle live on in memory—wise, active, creative, loving, generous, supportive, caring, sweet people."

Nat Jr.'s contemporary, as his father had been to her mother, John worked in theater for many years before moving back to Hurricane Hill. He has written a book, *The Day the Music Died*, and more recently he created *Whispering Waters*, a video history of the Ozarks, which includes some of his Aunt Nat's home movies of Camp Carry-On at Mountain View.

The next letter was written by Edwin Langdon Hanna of Spartanburg, South Carolina, cousin of Nat and once the owner of Camp Greystone, upon the death of her brother John Wilson in September of 1978. This letter relates the deep connection with another of the Wilson siblings. Written to Mary O. Shattuck, it was shared with Natalie Jr.

Dear Mary O.

To learn that my first—probably only—Hero no longer lives distresses me very much. Although he was an upper teenager when I was summering at Hurricane Hill, I thought him GOD. But no wonder. He took me fishing in Bear Creek; took me with him and Tango on all the errands in the buggy; took me with him and the Episcopal Rector to the Old Quarry to Swim (in the nude!) Where he lost his treasured Rod and Reel when he had to grab me when I fell and almost went through an old railroad trestle, which was the approach to the quarry. And then the stories he told after we had crawled through the window to our bed on the sleeping porch. And he played pool with me—built me a swing, and much more. This is all quite amazing. Had an 8 or 9 year old cousin been dumped on me when I was 19, I'd probably left home.

John was also a very special hero to his Aunt Kate. Her quotes from his early years are part of Our family jargon. And his letters to her. (Imagine corresponding with your Aunt!) Were a joy. I'm so sorry for you and Nat. I've never known anyone who was such good company. Virginia joins me in sending you, Nat, Max, Little Nat, and Steve our Love. Edwin

Note: When Nat was eleven, her Aunt Kate gave birth to baby Edwin. Due to complications, Nat was sent to Brookfield to look after both baby

and mother for several months. Elma's youngest sister was a favorite of all on Hurricane Hill. Kate and her family remained close to Nat through the years.

Virginia and Edwin Hanna wrote a letter of condolence to Nat Jr. upon the passing of Big Nat:

Dec 22nd, 1986

Dearest Nat, "Joe" [Edwin] and I were deeply distressed when your letter came telling us of Nat's death—It did not seem possible to us that we had not realized she was as ill—and that one so vibrant and vital should be gone. It seemed to hit Joe very hard—as his childhood memories of Nat and of John meant so much to him. And my memories stretch back to the early 30s when we first married and visited Hurricane Hill. And later having the privilege of having Big Nat and you at Camp Greystone. Those were happy days and we cling to the memories. The beautiful letter you enclosed—a real and heartfelt tribute to Nat brought tears to our eyes. You've certainly inherited the fine ability to write expressively."

From Lem Shattuck, Nat and Max's grand great nephew [sic], the pilot

Hurricane Hill in Warrensburg, inhabited by my maternal grandmother Mary O. Shattuck, was the one constant feature in an other-

Baby Edwin

Natalie Jr and Edwin Hanna reunite in 1987

wise unsettled early life for myself, my brother and my sister. We spent every summer in the sprawling Victorian house where she lived with her brother, John, my great uncle and next door to her sister Nat, my great Aunt. Hurricane Hill could be described as a family compound, originally occupying almost 10 acres adjacent to town with outbuildings and a barn. The Barn contained objects of power and significance to a child, such as a mummified cat in the loft. The summers passed in an idyll of the scent of lilacs, catching fireflies and heroic safaris with a Daisy Red Ryder BB gun. But I spent most of my time with my Aunt Nat's husband, Max.

Uncle Max and I got into his old Dodge pickup every morning and travelled at a stately 20 miles per hour to his farm five miles east of town where he raised Hereford cattle. Max was not given to a lot of idle chatter, in fact he could fairly be described as taciturn, and we would ride in companionable silence. Once at the farm he would saddle up Colonel and Rex and we would ride into the soft morning to look for newborn calves or sometimes, just to ride. After the horses were brushed and put away the work of the day would commence which was varied and always intensely interesting. We might drive the cattle to the barn to doctor them, spray the road ditches with the tractor and spray wagon, maintain equipment, or I might buck bales of hay behind the clanking New Holland square baler as Max crept down the windrow pulling baler and wagon with the International Harvester 300 Utility tractor. My favorite job was mowing pasture with either a rotary mower or sickle bar mower. Max would mow the outside swath to mitigate the very real possibility of an eight year old tearing out one or more sections of tightly strung fence then sit me on the tractor to spend the rest of the morning, or day, happily making decreasing rounds until the bunnies made a break from the last stand of hay in the middle.

While all of the folks on Hurricane Hill were individuals of remarkable attainments, those of Max resonated most strongly with me. He was trained as a civil engineer and I regarded him as the high priest of the skills I deemed important then and, to a large extent, still do. He could work in leather, wood, earth or iron, was accomplished with the stitching pony and the forge, and the products of his effort were always done correctly and meant to last. He was emblematic of the traits, highly lauded but now largely absent, of industry, self-sufficiency, and toughness.

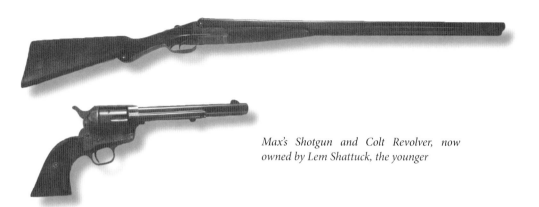

Max's Shotgun and Colt Revolver, now owned by Lem Shattuck, the younger

Max served in the First World war in the 129th Field Artillery E Battery, in the same battalion as Harry S Truman, dragging 75 millimeter field pieces and caissons through the mud of France with mules. It occurs to me now that if there was an experience calculated to instill a certain amount of reserve in a man, that might be the one. There were special times, though, when his reticence evaporated and those are still my most enduring link with him back through the years.

Max loved firearms at an early age. His daughter, my cousin Natalie, gave me his Remington double barrel 12 gaugeshotgun several years ago. There is a handwritten note from Max as a very young man contained in the butt stock that says: "Warrensburg, Mo. Dec. 20, 1911—

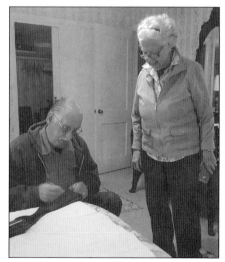

Dear Reader: This gun belongs to Max Prussing of Warrensburg. Please take good care of this gun as all former owners have done. Respectfully yours, Max M Prussing".

Max was an avid shooter, reloader and collector. To Max a firearm was a tool but one that, as any fine tool, can be admired for its own sake. On some special evenings the large canvas bag that held his hand guns would come out from the closet and Uncle

Lem and Nat remember the note Max had hidden over 100 years before

Max became as close to effusive as I would ever know him. I eventually learned by heart the catechism of the Smith & Wesson Model 1 bottom break, the Navy Colt, and the Single Action Army, each with its history and story. He still had his Model 1917 Colt service revolver from the World War complete with half moon clips and lanyard ring. When I asked him if the Army didn't want it back he unassumingly apprised me that he had taken one from a dead second lieutenant that did not seem to require his any longer and turned that one in when he mustered out. A mightily impressive answer for an impressionable kid and, come to think of it, I'm still pretty impressed today. Max as an adult was true to the ethos of his boyhood and the weapons were handled with jersey gloves and lightly oiled prior to being returned to their repository.

As a surveyor and engineer, Max was instrumental in the Lake of the Ozarks project as well as the construction of Ft Leonard Wood, later serving as the base engineer. He developed the town plan for Camdenton. He designed and built the buildings for Captain Nat's two campgrounds and more. Altogether, an impressive resume for a farm kid from Johnson County.

I am fortunate to have had as a role model the type of man that literally built America, competent, versatile, industrious and resilient.

From Evelyn Horner, St. Louis, MO 8/10/16

I have many fond memories of Natalie Wilson Prussing. She was smart, industrious, and sensible with a razor sharp wit.

I rode in a truck with Natalie and her namesake daughter, Natalie (Jr.) on their farm during calving season. When we found a newborn calf, the younger Natalie and I would get out of the truck. My job was to keep the calf down while Natalie ear-tagged it.

One particularly large calf was hard to pin down and the cows nearby came to "save" their calf. Using a stick I tried to keep the cows away as Natalie struggled to tag the calf. After finally tagging the calf we returned to the truck only to hear the elder Natalie say: "Girls, I could have sold tickets to that show!"

From Judith [Judy] Banta Cammack — 2016

I came to know Natalie Wilson Prussing through her daughter Nat Jr. The younger Natalie and I met sitting side-by-side as sopranos the first year for Warrensburg's Community Chorus in 1974. Many Tuesday evenings were happily spent in each other's company. It did not take long for Nat and me to feel connected as we have ever since, through thick and thin.

Nat learned in 1974 that my tween daughter was fixated with horses so most Saturday mornings promptly at 9 a.m. daughter Janelle hurried out to Nat's car at the honk for the short trip to the Prussing Farm on Montserrat Park Road where horsemanship, care and joy were experienced. Those times earned Janelle a job as a wrangler at a Colorado dude ranch for two summers after high school graduation and also enabled her to own a horse for her own daughter while living in Kansas.

Through these years I was often in Nat Jr's Little House on Hurricane Hill which was the home where she grew up and where her parents lived. Over the years I have known her cousins and an aunt.

Big Nat was unlike any woman I have ever known except for the qualities she instilled in her daughter: perseverance, common sense, independence, strength of character, humor, a sense of adventure, and fearlessness. I learned the stories of her striking out on her own in her educational pursuits and succeeding and forging new ground for women. You will have read elsewhere about her travels far distances in less than ideal circumstances (covered wagons and buggies) and relishing it all as a child. The hardships were not hardships for her. She was immersed in nature and gifted with a strong mind and body. As a young woman she had the advantage of European travel and experiences many of us can only envy.

Natalie was responsible for establishing Camp Carry-On for girls that surely changed their lives and their children's lives for the better. She threw a rock in a pond and the circles ever-widened.

She was civic minded as well, serving her community as chairwoman of the Johnson County Republican Committee and was a respected leader. She was honored at the first Annual Lincoln Day dinner in 1979 as the grand "young lady" of the Grand Old Party.

Cautious, and determined, Big Nat put her blonde two-year old daughter on the back of horse and told her to ride, and ride she did. She had this child confidently climbing a tall ladder to a barn hayloft with the goal of a great view from the upper windows, of rolling hills, horses grazing, the purebred Polled Hereford herd, all while smelling the freshly cured hay. These experiences surely structured Nat Jr's life as an only child who was never alone. She had the whole world at her feet thanks to her independent-minded mother. Her dear father had chosen Big Nat for her qualities and did not attempt to stifle her in her pursuits. He was her partner. He had his own big life that meshed with the lives of his girls.

After marrying and working in NYC and Atlanta, Nat Jr. and her husband Steve built their home in Warrensburg, on Hurricane Hill. There were two homes there originally—the little house and the Big House now occupied by Cousin John.

The two Natalies enjoyed traveling together and had memorable trips, including one to Texas so her mother could see the famous Blue Bonnets, which she loved, in bloom. Big Nat had fond memories of the years she had spent in Texas.

Over the years, Big Nat started to fade physically and eventually mentally. She did her best to maintain. She would sip down healthy smoothies concocted for her: whey, protein, ice cream, fruit—so good you would want it yourself. She would say thank you sincerely. I only saw her dressed in her "at home clothes" which usually included overalls. She eventually gave up her bra for the comfort of au natural. Her hair was thin, but to my knowledge she never complained or made mention of her appearance or how she felt. She thought WD-40 sprayed on arthritic aches and pains fixed her right up. She once told Nat Jr. not to worry if she didn't sleep at night: "eventually you will sleep!" That about sums up her solution to most problems: eventually things will work out one way or another; just make the best of it and keep going.

Drawing of Wilson House on Hurricane Hill drawn for and published in the W.H.S. Art Club Calendar by Nicki Dalhouser

Wilson Home on Hurricane Hill 2017

As the health of her parents failed, Nat Jr. took over the operation of the farm. Nat Jr was able to hire competent in-home caregivers for her parents over the years as they aged. She was vigilant in knowing how things were going across the yard between the two homes and that was the key to her parents' happy lives during their last years. I knew these caregivers, too, and they added color to our friendship. One funny story often retold in the family is when Big Nat and Max were ailing in their lovely sunny bedroom each in their own twin bed. Max had a visit from Dr. Folkner who called for an ambulance as Max needed hospitalization. As Max was being wheeled out of the room by the ambulance crew Big Nat remarked, "Did the old man have family?"

There was the time aging Big Nat saw a photo in the *Daily Star Journal* of a cat at the shelter who needed a home she called the shelter and "ordered" her. This beautiful long-haired yellow cat was delivered to her doorstep and was a fixture in the house until the end came. Mrs. Prussing in her mental decline was certain she had cats... plural, not just one cat. Cat darted here and there and thus her conclusion. We were all certain she would fall over the dang darting cat, but she never did.

For some reason I was accepted and welcomed into this family circle. I, too, had been an only child most of my childhood, so maybe my independence and confidence served me well in this friendship. I could pop in whenever (we did not live far apart) for a visit or to be helpful in some way. I was called by Nat Jr. on Saturday, October 25, 1986, to come sit at her mother's bedside while she ran an errand. Nat JR and I knew the end was near, but we did not know how near. (I was a baccalaureate nursing student then at UCM and graduated that December.) The short time I was alone with Big Nat was the time she easily breathed her last. I was holding her hand. No words were needed or spoken. Soon Natalie Jr. returned, special moments together and then phone calls were made. What a gift I was given though one I did not anticipate or request. Isn't that the way with grace? I can picture that bedroom scene as clearly as if it were yesterday.

Proverbs 27:20 says, "Better is a neighbor who is nearby than kindred who are far away." In the absence of my own parents who were far away, I know the truth of this scripture. These are my notes of the strong woman I loved and was able to share with my own children as they grew up and out. I still keep her close to me in memories after 40 plus years. If she were reading this she would brush it all off as nothing extraordinary and go on about her business of living. —Judith Banta Cammack

Excerpts from Sue Sterling's "The Saddle Bags Love a Long Trail Ride" — *Daily Star-Journal* —Thursday, October 9, 1997

They come from diverse backgrounds, and they may disagree on what to call themselves, but the members of "The Saddle Bags" an informal group of middle aged, and more than middle aged women trail riders are in total agreement about one thing: they love a long trail ride on a gaited pleasure horse. Natalie Halpin and Shirley Bryan are the two original members of the group. Halpin and Bryan met about 15 years ago at a trail ride sponsored by the Warrensburg Saddle and Bridle Club [of which Natalie was a founding member]. Each had gone to the ride alone and when they met they "bonded." They began going to rides together and the more rides they went to the more lone women they found." Banding together, the group grew and changed. The common "love affair" of these married women—whose husbands don't ride is the gaited pleasure horse. The group began as the Saddle Bags, but transitioned through several names. Halpin said with a laugh, "I'm not a Foxy Trotter. When I met Shirley I had not done much trail riding off the farm." Shirley had a similar experience and they found trail riding more their speed. "We used to ride fast, completing 20 miles in a morning. We don't go as fast as we used to."

The Saddle Bags, from left, Jo White, Shirley Bryan, Natalie Halpin, Phyllis Herzing, Norma Callahan, June Engel

Patsy and Nat Jr.

The women rode at state parks, conservation areas, and commercial horse camps. A tradition was the "Mushroom Ride" which started when they discovered a large crop of mushrooms along the trail. Thirty people were fed by this harvest at breakfast the next day. Unfortunately they never found that many again. Natalie would go on partial wagon train rides, usually for two or three days.

In closing Bryan said, "There's no waiting around, we never have to wait on the group". They had some memorable moments—usually ones we can laugh about—such as one ride in which Halpin fell off in the river. And Halpin added, 'We have been lucky. We really haven't had any bad experiences, but we're also very careful'.

While Halpin rode on her family farm as a child, she never had access to a trailer, just riding on the farm and helping work cattle. "

From Patsy Fisher Broughton, Louisville, Kentucky--May 31, 2016
Hi Nat,

Wow! How exciting for you. I am so impressed that you are writing a book about your Mom and thank you so much for giving me the opportunity to share some of my memories. And yes, it did start a flood of memories, not only about her, but about our amazing friendship of little girls growing up.

Some of the first things that came to mind were things like:

She taught us to play Canasta (and other games, I am sure)

She corrected my grammar (for which I am so grateful, wish she had worked on my spelling) Thank goodness for spell check.

She always allowed us to do crazy things, productions in the hayloft, climb and watch the stars from the top of a haystack after dark, stay in the "little house"

Nat, on the tractor as she often was, mowing the lawns and pastures of Hurricane Hill

all by ourselves. She trusted us to be responsible and make good decisions.

She invited Mom and I to "proper tea." Wow! That was new for us!

We watched her mow hay on a tractor, on the pasture across the road from us.

My Dad milked her cow so we all could have milk, cream, cottage cheese and butter. (I am quite sure she could have done that herself ... umm, maybe she just wanted us to have the milk, but knew that was the only way Dad would accept it.)

She worked it out for me to attend Girl Scout camp. Dad, Mom, Bob, Sharon (toddler at the time) brought me down to the camp in pouring down rain. Literally the creek rose and they were trapped for the night. Do you remember that?

When Sharon was born, your Mom carried you on her back down to see my new baby sister, (you had broken your leg at Christmas, just a month before, riding down the lane to show me your new bicycle.)

Nat your mom was non-traditional (when I compared her to mine) and absolutely exceptional, a lady before her time who could literally do it all with grace and integrity. Looking back on those days, I have no way to know how much she influenced me, but quite a lot I would imagine.... I am thankful for having both of you in my life...

Love, Patsy

From Pam Dickmann, June 2016, Kentucky

Mr. Prussing was bigger than life... to me.

First, he was Natalie's dad (Nat Jr. being a friend who loved horses and riding as much as I did) and secondly, he had what was considered the biggest mule barn in the state. In the 70s, in my mind, that was big stuff.

But he didn't like mares … only geldings on his place. I, of course, had a mare named Cile who was family and went everywhere Nat & I rode.

I don't remember the why (I've slept since then), but I needed to board Cile and asked Nat if Cile could stay at the Prussing Farm. Expecting a "NO" because of her gender I was surprised she was allowed on the property. Nat's gelding, Toby was in love with Cile and protected her and followed her everywhere. He was happy she could come and stay in his home pasture. Then one day when I was at the Prussing house I saw a bird feeder hanging in the bushes outside the kitchen window with Cile's name and horse shoe on its roof. I don't remember if I gave that to Mr. Prussing as a thank you for letting Cile stay on his farm, or if he made it. Just seeing it hanging in such a prominent place let me know that Cile had made it into his heart … even though she was "a girl." I loved him even more for that.

From Norma Jean Grainger, January 23, 2016

I first met Mrs. Nat Prussing in the early '60s at the Republican Headquarters on Railroad Street in Warrensburg. I had grown up in a non-political "vote for the best person" family but married a strong Republican. So… I had a question about a Republican candidate running for a county office that I wasn't sure I wanted to support. I stopped by with my toddler daughter in tow, and intended only being there long enough to ask my question. I found Mrs. Prussing writing campaign letters and she graciously answered by question and talked at length about so many things and soon I found myself and my daughter stuffing campaign envelopes. I was so in awe of her intelligence, her political and non-political interests, her talents, plus her gentle spirit…. The toddler is now a journalist and magazine editor and her daughter is also a writer. They wouldn't approve of my sentence structure, etc… so we won't tell them… Best wishes, Norma Jean Grainger.

From Virginia Young, 4/13/2016

When a person my age says that another individual is a "force," the word is followed with "to be reckoned with," the implication being that some sort of conflict is involved. This is not the case with Mrs. Natalie Wilson Prussing, affectionately known as "Big Nat." Of course, this statement needs clarification: When Jim (my husband) and I first moved to Warrensburg in 1968, I was almost immediately invited to join the Johnson County Republican Women's Club. I have no idea who invited me. The person in whose home I remember meeting the most frequently was Bertha Hursh on South Street. I don't remember if Mrs. Prussing was the president. However, it was understood by all without the fact being mentioned that Mrs. Prussing was the leader in terms of accomplishing the work of the Republican Party. Mrs. Prussing was a force.

Oddly enough, although Mrs. Prussing had power in the political sense, she had none of the aura of a powerful politician, ordering underlings about and constantly letting others know she was in charge. I never heard her tell anybody what to do, whether the task was big or small, but in her presence, things fell into place. Perhaps by the time I arrived in Warrensburg, Mrs. Prussing had been a leader for so long that the details had already been worked out. Whatever the source of this ability to manage quietly without fanfare and have events unfolds smoothly, it was Mrs. Prussing's gift to those with whom she worked.

Within the JCRW GROUP, Mrs. Prussing never seemed to pay attention to me; I never met with her privately or even in a small group. I did know that she had a daughter who lived and worked in Atlanta. When I heard that Mrs. Prussing was having a tea in honor of her daughter, Little Nat, who was returning to Warrensburg, I was surprised to learn that I was invited. I later found out that I had been identified as someone who would likely become a close friend to Little Nat. And that is the way it turned out. How much thought Mrs. Prussing had given the matter is something we will never know. However I think the uncanny way in which this happened was the secret of Mrs. Prussing's power. She had a special insight into how to make things work. This insight, along with her ability to get things done efficiently and effectively, with absolutely no struggle, no commanding posture, no raised voices, and no fussing—was the source of her FORCE ... (brand of invisible power).

Big Nat operated in the world of common sense. For her, life was too short to be concerned with things that do not really matter. She had a no frills personality. She was no fan of rigmarole or falderal. "Her world" was simply matter-of-fact in spite of the fact that her life experiences were quite astonishing—especially given her era—a side of her you will read about elsewhere in this volume. Here's an example, however of Mrs. Prussing's common sense attitude.

Natalie Wilson Prussing lived in practical realm where reasonable people function in a matter-of-fact manner. Acting unreasonable or sadly is a waste of time. And speaking of time, perhaps some of my impressions of Mrs. Prussing were part of the age in which I knew her. Those were days, when, if people were upset by something, they were much more likely than today to address the concern through old-fashioned problem solving based on reason and experience. What made all this work was a soft sense of fatalism and a strong sense of courage. Mrs. Prussing personifies this approach to life; she was a strong woman, a courageous person, an intelligent lady, with an uncanny skill for getting things done, comfortably, non-abrasively, and reassuringly. Mrs. Prussing was an ideal person to emulate. It would be impossible for any of us to follow her approach to life exactly in today's world, but learning to cope with life is much simpler when one handles problems with common sense, courage and confidence, using her example. Little Nat and I have never been quite up to the task, but we gained a good bit of know-how from Big Nat and that has made a significant difference in our lives. Ginger Young

From John Innes 8/1/2016
Dear Nat,

I'm finally setting pen to paper for memories of your mother. Apologies for the delay—I am no doubt taking retirement too seriously. Big Nat, especially before, but also during our time deserves several books and I am so happy that you and Lisa Irle are active in that direction.

Lots of memories, but they are seldom first-hand. Over our years growing up, I got to know your mother from your own frequent observations (and later from your excellent writings.) Memories of Big Nat came early on from my own mother who—from her childhood and from her own mother—knew slips and shreds of the biography that you and Lisa are assembling.

My mother was also active locally in Girl Scouts and found herself surprisingly enlisted by your mother for camp kitchen duties at Montserrat Park. Our mothers shared an ongoing concern for Republican Party activities, and I do personally remember your mother's being a convention alternate delegate and describing her meeting with Senator Barry Goldwater. This was an authentic big deal, as he would initiate a re-defining of Republicanism in his book, *Conscience of a Conservative*.

My first-hand recollections: [these continue the memories of John Innes]

Your mother defined Hurricane Hill (as did her siblings John and Mary O.). When I was a young child I was invited there for campfire and roast marshmallows or something. Gathered around the fire, we were impressionable, as ready for experience as your mother was to instruct and lead. Whatever other benefits were offered, I have never discarded my principal from that experience that we could sometimes avoid too much smoke by getting nearer the fire. Even now I "hear" your mother's voice in that practical admonition.

Later, my first (and should-have-been-last) horseback ride was promoted and hosted by yourself and by your mother. The horse was Colonel, and the place was your expansive pasture enclosed by the rustic split rail fence. Colonel did not seem understanding, and wanted no part of me. I fell off rudely and unexpectedly and your mother was practical in helping after the upset.

As we approached young adulthood, your mother and father sponsored an evening's Little House gathering of future partiers, and this seemed to reveal your mother's philosophy as nudging us into a sponsored by well-regulated life transition. It was a new and uncertain social adventure to me, though not to my more worldly visiting cousin, Anne, who was at ease and appreciative. My salient memory here was hearing the popular Hit Parade number, "Shrimp Boats" (is a coming, their sails are in sight.... There's dancin' tonight....) It was equally impressive that you had sound equipment! Along about these times, or probably a little earlier, I remember that your Mother and Father let you have a real working exclusive phone with Patsy Fisher—from your bedroom across the fields to her house. Your mother's equanimity was inspiring and probably assumed that you two would not violate international moral standards in your confidence sharing.

Big Nat's childhood freedom during an Idyllic year in the West (with relatives and her own Indian pony) may well have influenced her later parenting approach. As we all emerged from 4th-6th grade and junior high—you and John were free and brave enough to pioneer the July Fireworks sales world. (You and John graciously included me and then more of our siblings and cousins, and ultimately even Hugh Hanna following his own fireworks disaster.)

More than was truly necessary, we tooled about in a WWII white Jeep, (finding spots and setting up or gathering more stands (yes, even at Dale Ellis' Top Hat Nightclub), adding partners, enduring windstorms and rowdies who tossed Bulldogs, TNTs, etc. into the stands. Other super-friendly and I'm sure well-oiled spirits caroused about with lighted Roman Candles.

Then, on Hurricane Hill, itself, there were the celebrated Voo Doo Parties—when sometimes irresponsibly, we may have extended the party from the Little House to your parents' home—most probably while they were trying to—or pretending to—sleep.

Yes, these are memories of our growing up, and not directly of your Mother. Thus my recollections are usually of her monitoring at a prudent distance, probably entertained, and ready to help if needed. I was gloriously unaware of any parental anxiety, though in retrospect ALL of our parents –certainly including your own patient and no doubt forbearing mother and father earned sainthood along with a bit of premature aging. In all of this, Big Nat was always to me generous and well-wishing, presiding in the background helpfully and without interference. When I gave a piano recital before leaving for college, it was not exactly glorious, but your mother was so supportive in attendance and gracious at our home afterward.

I think—earlier than might have happened—we slipped some bonds of normal family supervision. While extending our adventures and explorations to the Quarry outside of town, to Kansas City's Starlight Theater and afterwards nightlife, and to Branson when it was more authentically itself—we really weren't dangerously irresponsible.

To the credit of your parents and mine, they understood this—according to us quite a childhood! I've got to stop. To review this is to forever re-do. Continuing good thoughts, Nat.

Much Cheer, John Innes, Spokane, WA

Natalie Wilson Prussing excelled at just about anything she tried her hand at. That included cooking, so here is one of her well-remembered recipes. Apple trees were near at hand, so no running to the store was required.

Nat Wilson Prussing's Applesauce Cake

Prepare and mix the following:

1 cup sugar

1 ¾ cup flour, sifted

1 cup raisins

1 cup black walnuts

Mix these ingredients and add to the above

½ teaspoon salt

1 teaspoon cinnamon

½ teaspoon cloves

In a pan on *LOW heat:*

1 cup apple sauce (best if homemade from stolen apples)

½ cup butter

1 teaspoon soda

Cool a bit and stir in one egg.

Stir moist ingredients into the dry. Pour into greased cake pan, prefer-ably tube or bundt.

Bake at 350 degrees for 45 minutes or a little longer.

A fond farewell, Camp Carry-On.

Resources

Archives of Natalie Wilson Prussing

Writings of Natalie Prussing Halpin

Columbia University Archives, NYC

Sargent College Archives, Boston, MA

University of Central Missouri, McClure Archives, Warrensburg, MO

University of Missouri Archives, Columbia, MO

Warrensburg Daily Star Journal

Columbia Missourian

Paul Bass, *Ft. Leonard Wood*, Acclaim Press

Recordings by James and Virginia Young

Lem Shattuck

Service Command Conference, Pictorial Review, Repairs and Utilities Activities –Post Engineer, Fort Leonard Wood, MO 27,28,29 July 1944" "Prepared by direction of Headquarters, Army Service Forces.

ABOUT THE AUTHORS

Natalie (Jr.) Prussing Halpin's intention when she began writing stories about her parents was to introduce the world to two incredibly kind and hard-working individuals who had excelled in adventurous and groundbreaking careers, never seeking recognition. Educated in her home town and at University of Arizona in Tucson, Natalie Jr.'s journey would lead her to a fashion career in New York City and an FBI agent she would marry. Like Captain Nat and Judge Max, her path would eventually lead back to the beautiful Hurricane Hill where she grew up and the Prussing farm four miles away. She has happily exchanged "pearls and high heels" for "cowgal boots and bandanas."

Natalie Jr. has recorded her memories of family stories, and also of her own upbringing. She joined the Warrensburg Writer's Circle in order to perfect her writing style so the inspiring lives of her parents might inspire others. The roots of her lifelong love of horses and the farms she still frequents will become apparent in these stories.

Lisa Irle, author of two books about the history of Warrensburg, Missouri and Johnson County, is a graduate of McPherson College and received a Master's degree (M.Ed.) from University of Missouri-Columbia. An avid reader, Lisa was a bookseller for several years. Her tenure as the curator of the Johnson County Historical Society lasted for 16 years. In addition to caring for the collections and assisting patrons at JCHS she often served as editor of the newsletter, directed historical reenactments and worked to encourage the preservation of local history through writing, music, and drama.

Natalie Jr. asked Lisa's assistance to organize her stories and design and implement the project of completing her book. This included sifting through and digitizing or transcribing ephemera of the lives of the Wilsons, Prussings, and Halpins. Lisa researched outside sources, as well, and wrote intervening passages connecting the stories and memories of this talented and beloved family.

INDEX